LOVE
TRIANGLES

LOVE
TRIANGLES

SEVEN STEPS TO
BREAK THE SECRET TIES
THAT POISON

LOVE

DR. BONNIE JACOBSON
WITH GUY KETTELHACK

Produced by Skylight Press

Crown Publishers, Inc.   New York

Published by Crown Publishers, Inc., 201 East 50th Street,
New York, New York 10022. Member of the Crown Publishing Group.
CROWN is a trademark of Crown Publishers, Inc.

Manufactured in the United States of America

Library of Congress Cataloging-in-Publication Data

Jacobson, Bonnie, Dr.
Love triangles : how to break the secret ties that poison love /
by Bonnie Jacobson with Guy Kettelhack. — 1st ed.
p.   cm.
1. Love.   2. Intimacy.   3. Interpersonal relations.
I. Kettelhack, Guy.   II. Title.
BF575.L8J27   1990
646.7′7—dc20   90-46616
                                                CIP

Book design by Deborah Kerner

ISBN 0-517-57711-9

10 9 8 7 6 5 4 3 2 1

First Edition

To my grandmothers,
Elizabeth Andress and Leah Singer,
who never gave a second thought
to what they were entitled to accomplish.

They influenced me,
by the way they conducted their lives,
to reach for it all in my own life.

CONTENTS

ACKNOWLEDGMENTS

Among the forces, triangular and otherwise, that have influenced this present creation, I would particularly like to thank Rose Singer, who has taught me most of what I know about loving and loyalty; Charles Singer, who gave me the basic foundations for role boundaries and commitment; and Arie Shapira, Eric Jacobson, and Brad Jacobson, for an opportunity to practice what I learned. Thanks to this present volume, they are unflinchingly confrontive whenever I attempt to triangulate them—a sharp reminder of how easy it is to do. I also thank Lynn Sonberg, Meg Schneider, and Guy Kettelhack for showing me how fruitful and productive healthy triangles can be, and finally, all of my lovely and sincere patients who are the font of much of the wisdom that I have acquired so far.

INTRODUCTION

I have been practicing psychotherapy for twenty years and been in the field of mental health since 1963. Obviously, after so many patient hours, I have been in contact with a very large array of people dealing with a myriad of experiences and problems. Also, all these years in one field have led me to be exposed to training in just about every discipline, from psychoanalytic and behavioral systems theory to spiritual, medical, nutritional, and biological theories. My healing methods, in regard to patients, are extremely pragmatic. Put simply, I try to give my patients both what they want and what they need. More often than not, this involves an exploration of what I have come to think of as their hidden love triangles.

The other night I was having dinner with my sister and brother-in-law, who were celebrating my sister's birthday. After uttering a particularly telling remark (though I hardly thought so at the time) about my mother, my family instantly pointed out how my own love and loyalty to my mother will always be a threat to my relationship with my husband. Here I am writing a book about love triangles and still I needed the outside observer to point out my *own* potential point of entrapment in the journey toward having a successful love relationship with a man.

Focus on the analysis of love triangles is one small pivotal point in the patchwork quilt of the multitude of forces that contribute to successful intimacy. But it is a crucial point because underlying all love triangles is the individual's resistance to separating from an earlier relationship. Becoming more conscious of this resistance will help you to be less fearful of intimacy. Using this one idea as a point of focus can help you to learn how to be more intimate, just as in learning any other skill. Think of learning a sport such as tennis. If you can train yourself to focus on one weak point in your game, it can bring your entire game to a higher level for more effective and pleasurable play. Although I realize that my continuing developing relationship with my husband depends on much more than mere awareness that I can feel disloyal to my mother if I transfer that deep and total love out of her camp to allow my husband to get in, it helps. Even now, as I am writing about it, it helps me to move closer to him.

This example of my mother and my husband and myself is a love triangle, but not the kind that usually comes to mind. Most people think that love triangles are affairs with sexual lovers. They are not always. Many family affairs actually block the possibility of sex between lovers. When parents are in conflict over their teenage son, when your mother-in-law is sleeping in the next room, when your law practice keeps you working until two in the morning, sexual love between partners usually suffers.

The purpose of this book is first to diagnose what your third presences are and then to assess if they are blocking your love relationship or, as they may be in certain cases, adding to it (not *all* triangles are destructive). You know that the third presence is constructive when, following contact, you feel more open to your partner. You know it is destructive when, after contact, you feel withdrawn, judgmental, or generally unavailable to your partner.

Love Triangles will teach you how to diagnose and assess the current relationships in your life, determine which ones help you to move forward and accept constructive change and which ones block you from growth and constructive risk-taking. This book is specifically designed to enhance your major love relationship, whoever your life partner is. However, it is also geared to instruct you about how to enjoy your number one love interest while maintaining satisfying and creative love relationships with others: parents, children, friends, and even business colleagues.

The last chapter teaches you specific skills for intimate listening. If you learn to use these techniques, you will be able to develop and maintain a one-to-one relationship with whomever you choose.

As you now begin your own private journey into the solitude of serious contemplation, I have an extremely valuable tool I wish to offer you as an accompaniment to this book.

Personal Journal

Before you even peek at chapter one, go out and buy a notebook for $1.99 because, if you keep a journal and use this tool in a consistent and conscientious manner as you work your way through *Love Triangles,* you can consider that you have entered psychotherapy with one of the best therapists you could ever find—yourself. Then this experience of self-discovery becomes a very expensive one—not in material terms, but in the expenditure of time. Even though you may be able to rush through *Love Triangles* in one, two, or three sittings, you will most benefit from this experience by giving it time. This journal-writing can be compared to farming. The writing is like tilling the soil. Once you loosen up the hard outer surface, you provide the space for unconscious thoughts and feelings to reach the surface of awareness. Then new forms of self-awareness can sprout. But this growth process takes time, energy, patience and dedication to change. If you decide to approach *Love Triangles* with journal in hand, you will truly be receiving an intense psychotherapy. You will also be offering yourself an outside observer because, very soon, the journal takes on a personality of its own. You will be quite enlightened by what you write down, especially if you return to reread earlier passages.

Not everyone is lucky enough or willing enough to have an outside observer experience with intimate partners, as I have with my siblings. But most of us can at least offer ourselves the opportunity for serious, self-respecting reflection. The journal then takes on the role of the outside observer. But no matter how you decide to approach the present volume, I hope you can at least feel my willing presence to take this journey with you. Good luck on this most interesting adventure.

LOVE
TRIANGLES

1

LOVE TRIANGLES

WHAT THEY ARE AND WHY YOU
NEED TO FACE THEM

EVERY TIME MARIANNE FALLS IN LOVE WITH A MAN, NOT TWO WEEKS INTO THE RELATIONSHIP she notices *another* man who she thinks might be better—and so she starts going out with him, too. When the first relationship breaks up, she soon finds the man she thought she wanted not as promising as the *next* man she meets. . . .

Al is so exasperated with his wife, Leslie, he doesn't know if their marriage can survive: he still loves her, but Leslie can't seem to make a single decision without getting on the phone to find out what her mother thinks. Al's beginning to think he married *two* women. . . .

Janet and Bob had a terrific romance, but now that Bob's pushing for marriage, Janet is suddenly cooling: memories of her ter-

rible first marriage keep popping up, and suddenly Bob seems
to be acting an awful lot like her ex-husband, Jack. . . .

What do all these people have in common? They're all involved
in love triangles. Perhaps this surprises you. Aren't love triangles
a clear-cut case of one lover "cheating" on the other—something
along the lines of wronged wife, philandering husband, and the
other woman? None of the relationship dilemmas above seems
to have much to do with that classic threesome.

In fact, they can be a lot more complicated than you may realize. Their permutations and effects can be bewilderingly
elusive—far more subtle than the B-movie scenario that probably comes to mind when you hear the phrase "love triangle."
Not only are they subtle, however—they are also extraordinarily
pervasive. In fact, my claim—and the claim of this book—is that
nobody escapes them. In some form and to some degree, *love
triangles affect all of us.* What's more, nobody escapes their damaging effects.

Certainly most of us are familiar with the pain of love triangles. And few of us are strangers to the notion that they can be
irresistibly alluring, erotic, romantic. However, the excitement
of "taboo" emotions, of love "stolen" in secret, of a relationship
charged with romance and eroticism, is not a feature of all love
triangles. In my clinical work with scores of clients, I keep bump-
ing up against love triangles at the core of most of our relationship problems. The men and women who come to me for
therapy have taught me that there's much more beneath their
three-way entanglements than most people ever realize. We
become hooked to "triangulating" for a wide variety of reasons—
reasons of which we're more often than not completely
unconscious.

That love triangles are pervasive as well as compelling has been
corroborated in the work of other therapists and researchers; our
investigation into love triangles collectively makes it clear that

triangles touch and involve *all* of us in complicated and unconscious ways. Not only don't triangles have to involve outside sex to be damaging or depend on the other woman or other man to wreak their havoc—they don't have to involve what we commonly think of as an outside "lover" at all. They can involve anyone from your mate's mother, your father, or both your kids to either of your bosses or any of your best friends. In fact, perhaps the most general statement that can be expressed about love triangles is that they can involve *anyone* who is important in your life—past or present.

It's clear to me that we need to take a new look at our assumptions about love triangles—to investigate how we get into them, how they may be trapping us, and how, if we do find that they're crippling our ability to enjoy satisfying relationships, we might get out of them.

You've just opened the first book to give you that new look. But first, let's discover exactly what we're looking *at*.

▲
LOVE TRIANGLE: A DEFINITION

Given its wide range of manifestations, what definition can we come up with that applies to all love triangles?

Here's a simple, all-inclusive one: *A love triangle forms when two people in a love relationship become psychologically dependent on a third presence.*

"Presence" isn't just a fancy way of saying "person." The third "point" of a triangle isn't always a live human being. When, for example, Janet started to cool at Bob's suggestion of marriage, she was responding to the *memory* of her ex-husband, Jack—not to the actual man Jack himself. It's common for the third "point" to be a kind of "phantom" presence. This illustrates the first truth about triangles: they're not always easy to detect.

A second truth about triangles is that if you tend to "triangulate" (and we'll be offering you a full quiz to determine that in our next chapter), you're almost definitely in more than one kind of triangle. In other words, if you tend to have affairs outside your primary relationship, or tend to get involved with a partner who gets involved with other people, you probably are no stranger to love triangles that *aren't* so obvious. We'll investigate other categories of triangles (involving, for example, family members, "scapegoats," and "phantoms") later on in this chapter and throughout this book, but for now, be warned: triangulators typically triangulate in a much wider variety of ways than they think they do.

A third general truth about triangles may be even more surprising. Every triangle depends on some degree of complicity between or among its members. In other words, even in the classic case of wronged wife, philandering husband, and other woman, if the triangle continues for any length of time, I guarantee that each member of the triangle, even the wronged wife, to some degree *wants* the triangle to continue, whether consciously or unconsciously. This complicity can be very subtle, but it's almost always there. The point is, no one in a triangle is a total "victim": by agreeing to perpetuate his or her role in it, each member of a triangle at least tacitly agrees to keep the triangle going.

You can see from even this brief definition that love triangles can be pretty complicated threesomes. Our motives for getting into them and, even more, *staying* in them even when we "rationally" see they're destructive can be very slippery. But we can start to understand how and why we get locked into triangles by taking a closer look at the damage they do.

If you're in a painful love triangle right now, you don't have to be told some of the obvious ways triangles can hurt. The pain of rejection when you discover that your mate is having an outside affair can be devastating. If you're the one who is having the affair, the guilt you feel about "cheating" on your primary partner can be just as debilitating. Jealousy, resentment, anger, fear, insecurity—these are the common emotions love triangles engender.

Perhaps you have a history of getting involved with more than one romantic partner at once—or maybe you're in an uncomfortable triangle right now. Perhaps your mate keeps having affairs, and you want to understand why he or she keeps being unfaithful to you, or why you allow yourself to put up with it. You may also find that you can't seem to keep a parent or family member from meddling in your primary relationship. Or that the memory of an ex-lover prevents you from achieving satisfying intimacy with your present lover.

Each of these dilemmas involves a triangle, and each hides a host of fears, hidden agendas, and unconscious conditioning that take work to acknowledge and bring to light. That's an essential part of our task in this book: to uncover what's really motivating you to triangulate so that you can begin to see how to get out of the tangled and destructive threesomes you can't seem to help getting into.

But the greater goal is to bring you to a point where you can experience full, free intimacy with your partner—a fearless state of communion with another person in which you accept yourself as you are, and allow your partner to be who he or she is, too. This is far more achievable than you may realize—and you'll find that striving to attain it has a wonderful dividend. You'll discover you won't *need* to triangulate when you start to trust yourself and your partner in the ways you'll learn in this book.

We can't, however, reach these goals without taking some basic steps toward them. And the first step is to take a look at *why* we get into triangles in the first place.

▲
WHY WE TRIANGULATE

First of all, let's examine my claim that every single one of us has had to grapple with love triangles. Why do I say this? Because when you were born, you were born into a triangle. You, your mother, and your father provided you with the first social interaction you ever knew. It made you face a dramatic struggle: you realized you were suppose to love *two* parents—not only Mommy, but Daddy, too. The ways you learned to adapt to your first caretakers and the ways your caretakers taught you what was expected of you to get needed love and attention instilled patterns of response and expectation that continue to this day. In fact, no relationship you've ever been in or will ever get into *isn't* affected by that first, primal love triangle of you, your mother, and your father.

So, right off we can see the main reason every one of us learned to triangulate: we virtually had no choice! Attempting to please, appease, understand, and maneuver our way around *two* parents—in order to get the attention we craved—taught us some pretty potent lessons. And we've brought these lessons to bear on every subsequent relationship we've gotten into.

But if everyone learned to triangulate, why isn't everyone having affairs on the sly? Or participating in any number of other obvious and damaging threesomes?

While none of us escaped the effects of our primal triangles, those effects vary a good deal from person to person, and our urge to triangulate manifests itself differently in different people. Not all of the lessons we learned are "bad"—in fact, not all *triangles* are bad. But if it's clear that you do continually get into triangles that *are* damaging and that attack your self-esteem or keep you from experiencing full, fearless connection with a love partner, if you tend to cling to old behaviors even when you can rationally see that they're causing you damage, you obviously got the very strong message very early on that you couldn't *survive* unless you behaved in a certain triangular way. Your primal triangle (your two parents and you) instilled some especially fearful dictates that make you unconsciously believe you've *got* to triangulate to feel safe.

You learned to triangulate because you learned that three-somes can be useful. Take a look at the following list, and see why you may have found triangulating hard to resist.

▲

FIVE COMPELLING TRIANGLE GOALS

Triangles appear to promise to get us out of a number of difficult fixes. If you get into triangles reflexively, you're convinced on an unconscious level that participating in a triangle will bring you peace or safety by helping you in one or more of the following ways. Again, you're rarely *conscious* that these are your motives for getting into a triangle. But you almost always hope a triangle will:

1. Deflect anxiety and tension.
2. Help you to avoid intimacy.
3. Allow you to blame, or find excuses.
4. Enable you to mythologize.
5. Offer an escape from your feelings.

Let's take a look at what each of these unconscious triangular goals really means.

1. Deflecting Anxiety and Tension

When things seem to be getting too "intense" or difficult between you and one other person, drawing in a third person (or presence) can seem irresistible. In fact, as we'll see in more detail later on in this book, the *main* reason you triangulate is to ease the tension you feel with your primary partner. Deflecting the tension onto a third person or presence gives you a break from an anxiety you fear you couldn't tolerate otherwise.

2. *Avoiding Intimacy*

This follows from the above. When you're strongly convinced that intimacy is "dangerous," that opening yourself up to another person simply makes you too vulnerable to be "safe," it's common to triangulate—to find another person to lessen the pressure you feel in a one-to-one encounter. (Marianne and her string of men, mentioned at the beginning of this chapter, is an example of someone who uses triangles to avoid intimacy.)

3. *Blaming, or Finding Excuses*

Triangles are terrific for giving you scapegoats. When you're upset or depressed or unhappy, blaming it on "him," "her," or "it"—and going to *another* "him," "her," or "it" for solace—can seem very appealing. As you'll discover in a later chapter, sometimes the scapegoat that forms your triangle isn't even human: it might be a pet, or a hobby, or obsessive attention to your job. "It's all my mate's fault" becomes a very effective diving board into "That's why I have to turn to X—to give me what my mate can't give me."

4. *Mythologizing*

The impulse to "blame," so as not to have to look at what our own part may be in contributing to the dilemma, is a powerful one—and it can lead to some distorted role assignments in triangles. It's common to see everyone simplistically: your spouse might be the "villain," you might play the "prisoner," you may see a lover as the "savior." Good guys and bad guys, white hats and black—triangles give us rich opportunities to turn the people in our lives into larger-than-life adversaries in an allegory. The high drama we create is a very effective means of distracting us from what's really going on inside *us*. Which brings us to our final questionable "benefit."

5. *Escaping Your Feelings*

Triangles allow you instant escape from uncomfortable feelings—feelings that you're not equipped to face certain problems on your own. It's very common to turn to a third person, a memory, or an obsession whenever an uncomfortable feeling crops up in a primary relationship. Convinced (consciously or unconsciously) that you don't have the resources to face the unvarnished "truth," you flee to something or someone that can distract you from that "truth," help you to forget, to escape. The problem is, of course, that the problem that sent you scurrying away hasn't gone away itself. In fact, unattended, it usually grows worse.

These five triangular goals—which provide the most common reasons people triangulate—hint strongly at the desperation you feel when you seek to rid yourself of anxiety via love triangles. People don't complicate their lives in painful ways for fun. You triangulate because you feel, on some level, *you have no choice*. This is crucial to understand as we start out, because if you feel compassion for the part of you that fears change, you're more flexible—and more receptive to allowing positive transitions to occur.

The desperation behind the urge to triangulate can be so great, in fact, that it can take some fantastic and ingenious forms. Let's meet a young triangulator named Jeff who will illustrate one of the slipperiest of these forms, before we go on and get an idea of the whole range of ways triangles can trap us.

▲

MISERY ON A CONVEYOR BELT:
THE STORY OF JEFF

Jeff, good-looking and boyish at thirty-two, came to me because he was having trouble with the latest in a series of women he'd been dating, Lee. He couldn't understand why he always seemed to end up with "castrating" women—and Lee, he said, was one of the worst offenders. She was a high-powered, driven executive. "Lee has her life organized down to the last detail," Jeff told me. "She knows exactly what she wants and has very little patience with anything that blocks her from getting it."

What did Jeff find appealing about her? I asked. "Well," he began, "she's *beautiful*. I love put-together women, I guess, and Lee is certainly put-together. But I don't love women who put me down all the time—and Lee can't seem to help doing that, either. She keeps saying I'm not doing what I ought to be doing with my life. She makes it clear she thinks I'm a goof-off." Jeff paused, and looked up at me quizzically. "Come to think of it, that's how every woman I go out with seems to think of me. I'm just not—*ambitious* enough. The fact that I'm not spending every waking hour trying to be the next Donald Trump seems to bother the hell out of every woman I meet." Jeff let out a short, fed-up sigh. "I'm starting to think all women are cattle-prodders—that their main role is to nag men into being something they aren't. Maybe I'm just not meeting the right women. I don't know."

It turned out that Jeff was cooling on Lee, but he'd recently met another woman, Alison, who he thought might be "different." In fact, Jeff said, Alison *was* a little "nicer" than Lee. "She's not as tempestuous—she doesn't jump down my throat the way Lee does," he said. But Jeff had to admit that Alison was starting to get on his back about his "crummy job," too. It was also clear that Jeff was locked into a pattern of getting involved with two women at once: he admitted that he was almost always in a triangle "with one woman coming and another going."

It was clear that Jeff kept getting into a series of triangles with women that were reflections of one another. He was stuck in what was to him an exasperating rut—attracted to one ambitious, dominant, hardworking woman after another, all of whom saw him as "clay" they hoped to mold, raw material they felt they could whip into shape. "It's not only that I keep finding women like Lee and Alison," Jeff said. "They keep finding *me*. They seem to think I'm this guy with enormous potential who's just waiting for the right woman to push him to great peaks of success." Jeff let out another disgusted sigh—a longer, sadder one this time. "But I don't *want* to be a big CEO. The only thing I'm succeeding at is getting exhausted. And lonely. All I want is a woman who will love me for myself—not for the man I'll never be. Every woman I meet eventually makes me miserable, makes me feel I'm not enough. And I seem to make all of them miserable as well. I feel as if I should give up, get used to being a hermit or something."

As Jeff told me about his family, it became clear where his impulse to get into this particular rut came from. Indeed, as you'll see throughout this book, the triangles we're in today have very tight (if usually invisible) connections to our pasts. In Jeff's case, he was "acting out" his own poor self-esteem by finding women who would put him down. He was choosing women who would tell him outright what his own secret, inner voice (a voice he'd internalized from two cold and hypercritical parents) had told him over and over, throughout his life: "You're not good enough, and you'll never be good enough."

However, before he could start to deal with that internalized voice, Jeff needed to see how he was helping to perpetuate the rut he was in today. He needed to see it wasn't just "fate" that he kept ending up with the same kind of woman. He had to face up to the fact that *he* was choosing the particular women in his life for a reason, and that he was choosing to triangulate with them—making sure that one relationship always overlapped with the next so that he got as strong a negative message from them as possible. He also needed to see that he was perpetuating a pattern of behavior and response he'd learned from childhood conditioning—to see his dependence on this pattern compassionately, but to realize that now that he was an adult with resources he lacked as a child, he no longer *needed* to perpetuate it. That, in fact, it was the main obstacle to his enjoying true intimacy in his life today.

Through the exercises you'll eventually read about (and learn to do for yourself) in this book, Jeff was ultimately able to accomplish all this—to accept his triangulating urge, understand its roots, see why he "needed" woman after woman to reinforce the message he felt doomed to believe about himself, change some of the assumptions he held about himself, and alter his triangulating behavior. But the essential first step was to see the nature of the threesome that kept magnetizing him.

It was news to Jeff, at first, that he was even *in* a triangle—and it certainly was news that he kept himself perpetually rotating from one woman to another to satisfy his triangulating urge. In fact, the category his particular triangle falls into is one I call the Rotating Date Triangle. There are, however, other categories of triangle that can be equally hard to detect. In fact, triangles come in a bewildering variety.

We need to take a look at this variety for a simple reason: before you can investigate ways to get out of triangles, you have to see more clearly exactly what you're getting out *of.* So let's take a look at some basic triangle categories—categories we'll be exploring, chapter by chapter, in the rest of this book.

An important point: You may quickly identify one or two of the following triangle categories right off as something you're involved in right now. However, I can virtually guarantee that you have been or are now in other triangles you won't immediately be able to identify. As Jeff discovered, it takes some careful self-questioning before you realize that you're involved in some of the less obvious triangle forms. For this reason, I urge you to read about *all* of the triangle categories we'll cover in this book, even the ones you may now think don't apply. They'll help you to make connections you won't be likely to make otherwise.

▲
TRIANGLE CATEGORIES: A BRIEF TOUR

The triangulator's ingenuity is remarkable. As I've said, the third presence that completes a triangle doesn't even have to be present or alive to exert an influence. (In fact, the third presence of a triangle doesn't have to be human!) You'll gain even more appreciation of just how powerful the urge to "save" ourselves through triangles is from the following rundown of ways we triangulate. Each category will receive its own full chapter in this book.

The Lover Triangle

The Lover Triangle is perhaps the most familiar. It is the classic spouse/spouse/other person scenario, most stereotypically the wronged wife, philandering husband, and other woman. Rarely are all members conscious of their own complicity in this arrangement, but almost always that complicity is what keeps the triangle going. As we mentioned briefly before, even the "wronged" member of the triangle may unconsciously want the triangle to continue—he or she may depend on it to dissipate some of the "roving lover's" intimate demands, demands he or she doesn't feel capable of meeting fully.

The Phantom Lover Triangle

It's very common for the third element in a triangle not to be present. An internalized "voice" from a parent or other authority

(Daddy doesn't have to be alive to exert enormous influence right now) or the overwhelming memory of an ex-lover who has set a standard (good or bad) to which you can't help comparing your present mate can be an "absent presence" in Phantom Lover Triangles—an intrusive presence that interferes with you and your current mate, even if it is not there in body.

The Rotating Date Triangle

The Rotating Date Triangle can mean you, one "rotating" lover, and another "rotating" lover (as in Jeff's story)—and the logistics can turn into quite a juggling act. But it's also common for the rotating triangle to involve you, a "fill-in-the-slot" lover, and an internalized force—perhaps the disapproving voice of your mother, a disapproval she expressed about any man you ever met, or the fact that no man could be "as good as Daddy." Whatever way the Rotating Date Triangle manifests, it should be clear that its function is to help you to avoid intimacy and stay connected to some original person in your life that caused you to resist change.

The Members of the Family Triangle

Parents, grandparents, siblings—members of your family can be intrusive in some obvious and not-so-obvious ways. The third role is sometimes "traded off": sometimes a sister or brother will take the place of a parent to provide the third presence of a triangle. If you think of your family as a "burden," you can bet you're no stranger to this triangle. Anyone regarded as a "burden" is someone who is taking up space in your life—and your relationships. The hold our families have on us is tenacious, and far more subtle than you may realize. The denial we often have about the fact that we're *allowing* family members to intrude is usually considerable. It can take some careful sorting out even to recognize you're in a Members of the Family Triangle—or, even if you know that you are in one, you may not realize how many other family triangles you're prey to.

The Scapegoat Triangle

When I said before that the third presence in a triangle doesn't even have to be human, I was referring to Scapegoat Triangles. Sometimes the third "presence" in a triangle can be a career, an obsessive hobby, an adored pet, or the marriage of man and Monday Night Football—all of which can create triangular dynamics every bit as destructive and distancing as an extramarital affair. We are usually quick to deny that such "presences" are troublesome, that we're allowing them to intrude, that we're using them as excuses to avoid intimacy. In fact, they often become the source of great self-righteousness. The workaholic husband and the harried wife are commonly defensive: "But I'm only doing this for *you!*" In fact, they're almost always doing "this" for *themselves*—again, to avoid what they feel they can't deal with more directly: an intimate encounter with the primary love partner. When repetitive behavior becomes an excuse, you're probably in a Scapegoat Triangle.

The Healing Triangle

While it's true that triangles are often harmful because they enable us to avoid intimacy, sometimes they are actually beneficial for the same reason. There are times when it may be wise not to get too intimate, or at least to avoid confrontation, especially when feelings are high or undefined. Sometimes triangulating can momentarily relieve tension that you're accurately able to assess you cannot deal with in a direct encounter. Certain triangles—what I call Healing Triangles—can be useful adaptations. They may allow you to ease tension temporarily in ways that help you to get through difficult times. Other more permanent Healing Triangles can be wonderful additions to your life. Turning to a respected mentor or friend or therapist for a needed "second opinion" can enrich your perspective, creating "supplementary triangles" that can improve your life. Not all triangles are bad. Some, in fact, can be essential to your feeling of wholeness and well-being.

▲

FREEING YOURSELF FROM LOVE TRIANGLES: A NEW APPROACH

We've mapped out three general—and, it may seem to you at the moment, insurmountable!—problems about destructive love triangles.

One: Nobody escapes them.
Two: They're often extremely difficult to detect.
Three: We cling to them because we're convinced there is no better way to maintain equilibrium.

Much of the misery you may have experienced in relationships is the result of what can now be called obsolete triangular conditioning—lessons you learned as an infant or a young child that may have helped you to survive then, but do nothing but get in the way of your happiness now. The above three "problems" indicate three common and devastating effects of old lessons you learned before you had any idea there might be another way to look at the world.

It is a major task of this book to teach you to free yourself from this prison of conditioning—to extricate yourself from damaging triangular conditions and to control the reflexive reactions, based on old patterns, that cause you to gravitate to triangles. I'll show you how to become sensitive to your triangulating habits so that you can begin to become free of them. Your triangulating urge doesn't have to control you—

you *can* learn ways to keep yourself from being miserable in love. Once you've learned how to keep yourself from triangulating destructively, you'll understand much more than how love triangles block you and what steps you must take to get—and stay—out of them. You'll learn something that goes beyond improving your love relationships—you'll learn something that will address, and begin to change, your deepest feelings and assumptions about what's *possible* between you and the person you love.

▲
HEALING THE DIVIDED HEART

What you need to do, and what this book will show you how to do, is take a close look at the fears that "divide" your heart, that keep you from trusting one other person enough to allow you to experience nurturing intimacy with him or her. The process of healing the divided heart—of extricating yourself from destructive triangle dynamics—means learning to accept parts of yourself that you may have violently rejected. It means learning to *integrate* what may seem to be disparate, warring elements in you so that you can coexist with them.

You begin this healing process when you learn to *diagnose* what the real "ailment" is. This requires asking yourself some questions you may never have asked before. It requires looking past what psychologists call the "presenting problem"—the way you think of and speak about your stress (in this case, the outer dynamics and damage of your love triangle; for example, the way it's tearing apart your relationship, or keeping you from feeling fully committed to one other person)—to the real feelings and fears that are plaguing you and sending you into all of the tangled three-way imbroglios in your life.

I'll offer you a very concrete series of questions you can ask yourself to begin to untangle your motives for establishing the threesomes you create. And then, a little later on, I'll offer you a program which will show how you can actually diagram your feelings—within the roles you and the other members of your triangles play—so that you can achieve a clear view of what you're doing in a triangle and why. You will get the most from this experience if you begin a personal journal. The questions you find throughout the book and the diagrammatic programs are designed to stimulate your mind into gaining access to less consciously available thoughts and feelings. Keep a journal of your answers to these questions, as well as any other thoughts or feelings that emerge, because, when you finish this book, you will have a valuable document that will help you to become more centered—clear about who you are and what your point of view is.

Again, you'll benefit from investigating *all* the triangle categories we cover in this book, even those that at first seem to be foreign to your experience. As you've already begun to see, we triangulate more unconsciously than consciously—and I want to be sure you wake up to all of the ways you may be trapping yourself in unproductive threesomes.

But before we get to these categories, we need to do some groundwork—some specific digging to accomplish two important goals: first, to discover the extent to which triangles may plague you, so that you become receptive to the idea that you're *in* triangles you may not realize you're in; second, to educate you about the roots of common triangular patterns, so that you begin to appreciate that your current triangular behavior is intimately bound to your past. Then, in the bulk of the rest of this book, you'll examine specific triangle categories to find out where, how, and from whom you learned the particular triangulating tactics you can't seem to stop using today.

Formidable as these tasks may seem right now, I think you'll find them easier than you expect—even if the questions I'll ask you to ask yourself may reveal some surprises about your triangulating self.

First of all, let's investigate how involved you are in triangles *today*. In the next chapter, you'll take a triangle quiz that will probably make it very clear love triangles are a greater part of your life than you ever dreamed.

2

ARE YOU IN A TRIANGLE NOW?

B Y THE END OF THIS BOOK, WE'LL HAVE EXPLORED A WIDE RANGE OF TRIANGLE SCENARIOS THAT YOU may never have realized were triangles to begin with—and I promise that more than one of those stories will strike familiar chords in you. No one escapes some scarring from the experience of juggling our affections for Mommy and Daddy; the effort to please both can never be completely successful, and this lack of "success" almost always results in some lopsided ideas about what love means and how to get it that plague us later on in life. We all struggle to achieve balance: no one had a perfect baby-hood or childhood and we all have personal and interpersonal blocks. But those of us who habitually resort to triangular tactics to cope with stress and fear and anxiety—and that's a very large number of us, as you'll see—can profit by confronting the source of our urge to triangulate.

Do you tend to get into love triangles? Are you in one now, even one of which you may not be aware? Are you likely to get into one soon? Answer yes or no to the following ten questions and see for yourself. Use your personal journal to record any further comments or thoughts before you turn to the discussion of the questions.

▲

THE TRIANGULATOR PREDICTOR QUIZ

1. Do you think of any member of your immediate family as a "complete nothing"? Are you embarrassed when someone you care about meets this person?

2. When you are with your date, lover, or spouse in certain social situations, do you cringe whenever he or she speaks—do you wish you'd come alone?

3. Do you think "all men" or "all women" are back-stabbers—do you believe you can't trust them?

4. Do you find it hard to "let go" in bed—to feel sexually free with your mate?

5. Do you find that no amount of approval is ever really enough?

6. Do you bend over backward to avoid any kind of conflict?

7. Do you always fall for people who are unavailable?

8. Do you think of yourself as a failure or an underachiever?

9. Do you feel you're too much for your partner to handle—too powerful, too emotional, too difficult?

10. Are there certain people you selectively don't tell your mate about, even if your relationship with them is perfectly "innocent"?

This may seem like a strange bunch of questions—they may not seem terribly related to one another, and you may be skeptical about their connection to triangles. But I guarantee that if you've answered yes to even one of them, you're no stranger to the triangulating urge. The more questions to which you answered yes, the more probable it is not only that you've got the "urge" to triangulate, but that your life has been or is now full of triangular attachments, whether or not you're conscious of them.

Let's take a look at why I've chosen these questions—and why answering yes to them indicates a strong tendency to triangulate:

1. **Do** *you think of any member of your immediate family as a "complete nothing"? Are you embarrassed when someone you care about meets this person?*
Generally, if you feel someone in your family is a complete nothing who embarrasses you or for whom you have to apologize, you're projecting your own feelings of inadequacy—you're afraid that someone you care about will judge *you* because of the behavior of someone in your family. Because you don't feel you can let the family member in question just "be," you feel the impulse to explain or excuse him or her, and otherwise make an alliance between you and the person you're trying to "protect" from the family member's offensive behavior.

Whenever you feel the urge to defend or explain someone else, you are either trying to impress a third presence or covering your own embarrassment about "ghosts in your closet"—which means you are in a triangle. Remember that we triangulate because we seek to diffuse tension: allying yourself with a "something" against a "nothing" is a way of allaying the tension and fear that you may be taken as a nothing yourself if you *don't* make that alliance.

One of the general reasons we triangulate—a reason we'll explore in a variety of guises as we go on—is that we feel a need to "mythologize" someone, whether into an ogre or a saint. Often you see the person you've labeled a nothing as offensive because of an unconscious need to define yourself *against* someone in order to feel better about yourself. It's a home truth that we don't like in others what we fear we might be ourselves—

which is the kind of projection we fall prey to (and inflict on others) when we label someone a nothing, especially someone as close to us as a member of our family. The corollary is that we often idealize the person we've decided is a "something." If we need to transfer the fear and discomfort we feel about ourselves to a nothing, we usually need the flip side, too: identifying with someone we make larger than life in the attempt to see *ourselves* positively. What we're doing is something we do in every triangle: we're assigning exaggerated characteristics, within specific roles, to escape the hard work of discovering who others truly are—as well as who *we* really are. Facing all the pros and cons, the warts and the beauty, the true rounded reality of the people in our lives can be terrifying—and this is perhaps the single most important reason anyone does triangulate. Luckily, however, we can learn tools to combat that terror, drain the negative energy from our urge to mythologize, and help us gain freedom from it.

2. When you are with your date, lover, or spouse in certain social situations, do you cringe whenever he or she speaks—do you wish you'd come alone?
This is a variant of what we've just talked about: if you *regularly* feel embarrassed by your partner when you go out, you're more than likely projecting your own fears of inadequacy in the way we've just described. But this also means that you feel the need to put distance between you and your partner so that there's room for a new third presence. When we cringe at a partner's behavior in the presence of other people, we're sending out a message to those other people: "I can't stand my partner either—someone come over and help me!" It's a subtle way of laying the groundwork for triangulating. Wishing you'd come alone means wishing you were free to connect in new ways, ways not hampered by the presence of a partner. You feel the need to be more freely available—to *invite* a third presence into your life

(which doesn't have to be another romantic partner, although it might be; it could be a whole group of people, as at a party).

3. Do you think "all men" or "all women" are backstabbers—do you believe that you can't trust them?
Our prejudices are very revealing. "Received truths" such as "You can't trust a redhead" or "I'd never get involved with someone who didn't have an L in his name" are more than curious quirks of human nature: we *do* in fact "receive" these prejudices either through direct transmission, by learning them from our parents or society, or through a more individual and self-protective process. That second self-protective process instills some of our most powerful prejudices and can be hardest to detect and break down, since it *is* so self-protective. The notion that all men or all women can't be trusted is one you may cling to because unconsciously you feel that the world is unsafe. It may be (in fact, it very likely is) underscored by family messages—by a distrustful attitude your family has. But you cling to the notion, if you cling to it at all, because psychically it makes you feel safer, more protected. From a triangle point of view, it does something else: it makes sure *one* person can never be enough. If a person is untrustworthy by reason of his or her gender, there's not much you can do to make that person trustworthy! Whenever we find unalterable reasons to distance ourselves from someone, we create space for a third presence—in fact, we all but send out an invitation to that third presence.

What this means is that you may look for someone who is "less" of a backstabber (if you're convinced "all men are . . ."). Or you may turn your mother, sister, or best friend into that needed third presence. Our prejudices limit us, and our inner selves seek compensation for these limits. If you feel one sex or the other is untrustworthy, you have guaranteed that any relationship you get into with a member of that sex will become a triangle: there will always be the need for someone or something else to compensate you for the limits you have imposed on the relationship.

4. Do *you find it hard to "let go" in bed—to feel sexually free with your mate?*
It's not a coincidence that this question follows the one we've just explored. Letting go—whether of blocks you may feel about enjoying life or sexual inhibitions in an intimate relationship—means, above all else, *trusting*. Not trusting means withholding part of yourself out of fear—and when you've withheld something as vital and urgent as your sexual self, you're eventually going to resent "having" to hold yourself back. Tension builds, and it inevitably seeks resolution—often through the means of a triangle.

Feeling a split between love and sex and choosing (or fantasizing about) one partner for sex and another for "nurturing" love or security is enormously common—so common that we'll investigate it in more detail later on, and you'll see it crop up again and again in the triangle stories we'll explore in this book. It is so common because of the way most of us learned, as infants and children, to separate sex from love, typically seeing sex as secret, forbidden, or dirty and love as acceptable, platonic, and passionless. It's also common to unconsciously associate the "good" or "nurturing" love with your mother or father, adding an incest taboo that reinforces the split. That split is often related to feeling sexually repressed: something is telling you it's "strange" to respond passionately to your mate. You may, for a variety of other reasons (such as childhood sexual abuse), also have been conditioned to believe that it's not *safe* to let go sexually with a lover. One possible reason for splitting sex and companionship is, if your primary caretaker was overpoweringly possessive, you fear being swallowed up by giving everything to one person. You could be free sexually with a lover outside your primary relationship because the threat of being consumed is diminished. After lovemaking you escape—after all, you *are* married. But whatever the reasons for repression, it's setting you up for a triangle. Your pent-up feelings *must* have an outlet—a third presence to gravitate toward. This doesn't necessarily mean you'll take on a lover (although you may). You may simply find yourself obsessively fantasizing about someone else, or these sublimated feelings may fuel relentless "concern" for your children, parents, or best friend.

Comfortable sex can, I believe, be described simply: it happens when you feel you can *take* pleasure freely and unconditionally—when, like an infant at its mother's breast, you feel you can "get, get, get" and that you are naturally entitled to it. The moment you begin to worry about how a mate feels about your performance, you've allowed self-doubt to enter your mind, and you may yield to the impulse to rate yourself according to some imagined standard. At this moment, good, comfortable, enjoyable sex flies out the window. What this also means is that if you cease to trust yourself, good sex is impossible: not trusting means shutting down, and shutting down means you can't let go in that childlike way, freely taking all the pleasure you want.

Giving ourselves full permission to "take" in sex is liberating—it teaches us that *everything* can be pleasurable, including giving pleasure to someone else. Giving, in a sense, becomes taking: the joy of unconditional trust and surrender to your feelings about yourself and your lover often means it's no longer important who does what to whom. Few of us can claim that we enjoy intimate relationships that always operate at this level of trust; those of us bent on triangulating invariably find we operate *least* on that level of trust. It's not that a triangulator may not find "good sex" with a third party, but if he/she *needs* two relationships in order to satisfy sexual desire and the longing for nonsexual nurturing, he or she is operating from some painful fears—most saliently, the fear of opening up in a wide range of ways to *one* person.

5. Do *you find that no amount of approval is ever really enough?*
Seeking validation through other people's approval provides, at best, very precarious security. You quickly learn that you can't control other people's responses to what you do or who you are, as much as you may bend over backward in an attempt to manipulate them into giving you the "right" response. Even if you "succeed," you may find you don't trust your success. "He didn't really mean it" or "She was just in a good mood" or "They were just trying to placate me" suddenly pop up as the "real" reasons for why you only *seemed* to get approval. However, even when you accept that you've won the approval you were after, if your self-esteem depends on it, you'll always want more. No amount of kudos can fill the void. Outside approval is like Chinese food, according to some people: you're always hungry an hour later.

But why does an insatiable appetite for approval mean you're likely to triangulate?

Whenever you feel inadequate in a relationship, you feel a void that urgently wants to be filled. You need *help*—so you tell yourself—and it's likely that you'll reflexively grab onto a third force for that help. You're hungry for reassurance, for corroboration, or simply for some means of shedding some of the burden of responsibility you feel you can't carry on your own.

When you depend on outside approval to the extent that you can never get enough, what you're really telling yourself is that you'll never have the resources to feel complete without the outside world's approbation—a Catch-22, since (as you've probably been aware from your earliest years) that outside world *can't* fill the void. This wreaks obvious havoc in any relationship you may be in. Since you never feel you're getting the approval you need from one person, you'll quite naturally look to someone else to provide what's missing. You've conditioned yourself to look *elsewhere,* all the time, since you deeply feel that whatever relationship you're in right now is not enough. The only way of breaking this cycle is to confront the fear that puts the cycle in motion.

Doing that is a major part of our task—one we'll tackle in great detail as we go on.

6. *Do you bend over backward to avoid any kind of conflict?*
If you're terrified at the thought of someone else's anger or disapproval, if you'd do anything to "keep the peace" and you find yourself in a "mediator" role over and over again, you're likely to triangulate.

Conflict is never pleasant and few people welcome it, but when the prospect of conflict between two other people terrifies you it usually means you're unconsciously convinced that you won't *survive* their potential blow-up. If you feel this way, the urge to say or do exactly what you think the others need in order to keep peace will obviously be a mighty one. Bending over backward to avoid conflict often means learning to play peace-maker between two opposing sides—one of the clearest and, often, most exhausting triangles anyone can get into.

7. *Do you always fall for people who are unavailable?*
This is one of the subtler indicators of triangulating, because the "third presence" is almost always present only in your imagination. For years, Betty could not understand her attraction to married men: she seemed to have a paranormal ability to zero in on men who were attached, even when they weren't wearing the telltale ring. "It was as if I could pick up on whether they were involved with a woman even before they told me they were. And if they were, I couldn't seem to help myself. I fell in love."

Betty had read enough women's magazines and heard enough about "how we avoid intimacy" to have an inkling that she gravitated toward married men because she was "afraid of making a full commitment"—but she didn't understand *why.* "It's not as though I came from a broken family," she explained. "I mean, I know friends of mine who are afraid of commitment because their parents' marriages were so bad—they had such destructive role models that they didn't believe any relationship could last. But that wasn't the case with me. My parents have always loved each other—they're really devoted. In fact, my father is the model husband, devoted to Mom, to us kids, demonstrative. What better example could I have had?"

When Betty went into therapy, she began to see that it was actually the image of "perfection" she saw in her parents, and especially in her father, that was the problem. She began to see that in subtle ways her father had made disparaging comments about all of the boys she dated in high school—and she got a strong, if subliminal, sense that they weren't "good enough" because they weren't her *father.*

"I'm beginning to see now that my father goes everywhere I go—I keep him right in the center of my head." Betty couldn't go out with a man without that third presence subtly rating the man and finding him wanting. Her psychic solution was to seek out *married* men—men who would remind her of her inaccessible father, and yet with whom there was little chance she'd actually have to fully commit: since they *weren't* her father, they could never be good enough, and she could stay "Daddy's girl" forever.

When the third presence of a triangle is as subliminal as Betty's, it usually takes psychotherapy to reveal it. But you may nonetheless, on your own, begin to have an inkling now of what that third presence you're carrying around may be—what "voice" (which can be as intrusive as any actual physical human being) is interfering with your relationships. A personal journal is a good place to keep track of those "voices" so that you can identify them, make peace with them, and eventually get out from under their restraints.

8. Do *you think of yourself as a failure or an underachiever?*
This relates to our very first question about projecting buried feelings of inadequacy onto a member of the family. Sometimes

we don't bother to project, however. We sometimes find a curious cold comfort in clinging to the feeling that *we* are the failures or inadequate ones. But what does this attitude have to do with triangulating?

Again, when you feel incapable of meeting the demands of a relationship, you are going to look for help. And, again, that help can manifest itself in any number of third presences: a lover, a friend, a parent, a child—even an "enemy." In fact, it's likely you'll seek out an enemy as a third force: when you feel you're a failure, you often seek out people who will corroborate that view. It's common for people with this attitude to gravitate toward someone abusive. Why would you want this view of yourself corroborated? Because, for reasons I hope to help you discover throughout the course of this book, it's the view of yourself to which you were conditioned. It's the only "self" you were taught in the triangle of yourself and your parents, and you still believe unconsciously that it's the only self that can survive.

Women who become battered wives generally come from a family history of severe physical and mental mistreatment. Abuse became to them a sort of expression of "love"—or at least attention—and because that was the predominant recognition they received, it became the feedback they got used to and expected. The battered wife's triangle is typically herself, her violent husband, and an internalized aggressive parent. But you don't have to have had that obviously abusive a background to triangulate this way: we learn in far subtler ways, sometimes, that we're "not good enough," or "couldn't possibly succeed," or "don't have what it takes." This self-doubt always translates into being terrified of accepting responsibility for ourselves or for our part in any relationship. (If we believe we don't have what it takes, what other way could we feel?) When we urgently feel we need help, we are drawn to triangulate because that "third presence" offers quick-fix diffusion—a way to get out of the terrifying possibility that we might have to face things using only our own inadequate resources.

9. **Do *you feel you're too much for your partner to handle—too powerful, too emotional, too difficult?***
This question is almost the flip side of the one we've just discussed. Sometimes you feel the person you're with isn't "capable" of dealing with all of your facets. You may even feel, somehow, that if you let out all your "power," you'd destroy your partner— the force of your personality would simply be overwhelming. "I can't have an exclusive relationship!" Barbara, a high-powered entertainment executive, once said to me. "No man could be *enough*." Barbara was quick to point out that she wasn't talking about sex—it wasn't the physical part that she felt was inadequate. "It's just that I'm so many different people—artsy one minute, all business the next, quiet and moody now, roaring for a good time later. What one male could contain all that?"

It's exactly the fear that we can't be "contained" by one relationship that causes us to triangulate. Not that there aren't times when you feel genuinely limited by a partner: you may indeed be denying yourself needed outlets by sticking with someone who isn't equipped to share everything that interests you. But in Barbara's case, when she dug a little deeper she realized that her real fear was something different from feeling she was "too much." Through therapy, she discovered that rather than feeling *too* "adequate" for one man, she was secretly afraid that she couldn't be consistently, reliably loving to one man. She was really afraid that *she* wasn't gentle, loving, or feminine enough to please a man, and she sought through wild extremes of mood and behavior to keep from ever developing a strong one-way commitment, a relationship in which her inadequacies would be found out. Often the paradox is that when you feel you're "too much" what you really fear is that you'll be exposed as "not enough." And you reach out for a third presence to distract you: you triangulate.

10. Are there certain people you selectively don't tell your mate about, even if your relationship with them is perfectly "innocent"? Perhaps you "forget" to tell a primary partner about someone you have lunch with every other day, about someone you talk to regularly on the phone or look forward to sharing coffee breaks with at work. You catch yourself so that you don't say something like "That reminds me of what Stan and I were talking about today at lunch," because you realize that you don't very much *want* your lover to know about Stan. Not that there's anything *wrong*, exactly, but . . .

Sometimes it's uncomfortable to admit to yourself that you really are attracted to someone else—it would seem too threatening to acknowledge it, either because you consider yourself "married" or because you know how jealous your mate would be. So you "hide" these attractions not only from your mate but often from yourself. You know you *like* Stan, but, well, it's not *that* important, is it? And anyway, it's nice to have a friendship all to yourself—someone your "significant other" doesn't know about. There's even something a little exciting about that. Not that there's anything *wrong*. . . .

In fact, there doesn't have to *be* anything wrong with having the occasional "secret" friendship. But if you find yourself frequently being secretive about friendships, to the point that you consistently have some private friend on the side, however innocently, you're probably avoiding taking a look at some important feelings that *need* to be looked at. What there's no doubt you're doing—even if it may be hard to acknowledge to yourself—is triangulating.

You've learned a great deal about the forms triangles can take and the slippery motives that can underlie our getting into them.

Now it's time to take a closer look at the anatomy of a triangle—to begin to see how, by taking a fearless look at its components, we can drain a triangle of some of its negative power. The first surprise is that you're not, after all, dealing with *one* triangle when you confront what's going on in your particular threesome. Each triangle hides another deeper triangle— and *both* of those triangles need to be addressed if you're to have a chance of getting over them. The next chapter will show you what I mean.

3

THE ANATOMY
OF A TRIANGLE

Y OU NOW KNOW THAT IDENTIFYING
THE TRIANGLE OR TRIANGLES
YOU'RE IN ISN'T ALWAYS SO EASY.
However, identifying your current triangle isn't the only triangle
investigation you need to do. There are still other triangles, triangles beneath the ones you're currently in, that need to be
looked at.

The truth is, *any* triangle you're in today hides the roots of a
much deeper, very powerful, unconscious triangle. In effect,
you're caught in two triangles at once: two varieties of triangle
I call "root" and "apparent."

▲
ROOT AND APPARENT TRIANGLES

We've already spent some time delineating apparent triangles.
They're simply the triangles you're in right now. But the *root* triangle

is an even more slippery article. It is, as its label implies, a first-cause triangle: the triangle that provokes you to construct all the subsequent triangles in your life. It's the "source"—the paradigm that teaches you to triangulate in the specific ways you do.

Your most powerful root triangle is usually the "primal threesome" we identified early on—you, Mommy, and Daddy. But you can have other root triangles, too. They might include a grandparent, a parent, and you; a sibling, a parent, and you; a teacher, a family member, and you; a first love, your best friend, and you. Sometimes these root triangles are "branch" triangles stemming from and reflecting the first caretaking triangle in your life; but they are still models in their own right for later triangle-making. Indeed, they can be as powerful (and as subtle) as your original mother/father/child triangle.

As I've said, we know that apparent triangles can be difficult to detect. Even "obvious" apparent triangles have their secrets and involve motives we normally don't even guess at. But *root* triangles can be the most elusive of all because we've spent all of our lives being influenced by our history. It does not occur to us to question it. We are rarely aware of how much our family of origin has shaped our behavior. This is the key to why it can be so difficult to detect root triangular effects.

Because your motive in relying on a triangle is self-protection, it's understandable if you resist changing, questioning, or sometimes even identifying triangular behavior, whether apparent or root: you're too convinced you need it to survive. Remember that we learn to depend on triangles because we unconsciously believe they will help us to relieve anxiety we don't feel we can release in a one-to-one relationship. As a result, you often end up, in a sense, *creating* a lover or other third force in response to certain persistent tensions and fears (much as you may want to believe it was fate, chance, or good or bad luck). As you'll soon see, you also often depend on triangles to manage a very troubling split between sex and love (or passion and comfort). One of the most common reasons people triangulate is to satisfy the disparate urges for sex and nurturing—urges that you may not be able to reconcile in yourself, and thus cannot allow yourself to seek in *one* relationship.

Because these hidden agendas are so urgent, you can become marvelously "disciplined" in your triangulating. You may create a triangle by reflex—the reflex to "save" yourself—or to vent emotions you don't know how to vent in any other way. And when your attempts to protect yourself by triangulating get you into trouble (as they almost always will), it's no wonder if you're baffled: the deepest, most fearful part of you was only doing what it "knew" how to do to offer *comfort*—not to create more problems.

Awakening to your root triangles requires a special sensitivity—a sensitivity I promise you can develop and improve through practice, and through a specific method I'll divulge in our next chapter. But now let's look at some general patterns of responding to root triangles that may ring a bell for you, reminding you, perhaps, of how your own background has set you up for the apparent triangles in your life today.

We'll do this with the help of some well-known people who have triangulated in ways that memorably illustrate common patterns the rest of us fall into, too.

▲

FAMOUS FAMILY TRIANGLES
AND HOW THEY RELATE TO YOU

First of all, let's reiterate the most important truth about triangles: they are *universal*. Everybody is affected by triangular dynamics. The reflex to draw in a third presence to relieve anxiety is deep in all of us. Researchers Monica McGoldrick and Randy Gerson, in their fascinating study *Genograms in Family Assessment,* bear this out. "Under stress," they write, "two people tend to draw in a third, stabilizing the system by forming a coalition, the two joining in relation to the third." Gerson and McGoldrick are here drawing from the work of triangle expert Murray Bowen, and they conclude with him that "the basic unit of an emotional system . . . tends to be the triangle."

What exactly does this mean?

"Under stress"—meaning under *any* stress—we look for an "out"—for some way of relieving that stress. Gerson and McGoldrick make some persuasive hypotheses about how certain famous families—the Hepburns (Katharine, brother, and mother), the O'Neills (Eugene, et al.), the John Quincy Adamses, the Franklin Delano Roosevelts, the Kennedys, and others—dealt with stresses peculiar to their backgrounds and circumstances. The model they use for exploring these families is one called a "genogram," a sometimes complicated but revealing interlocking pattern of parents, relatives, and children throughout several generations. While their express purpose was not to illuminate root triangles in these families, some fascinating root triangles nonetheless emerge from their speculations—triangles that illuminate both root and apparent triangular dynamics common to the rest of us.

Please do not regard the following as immutable "truth" about John Kennedy, Katharine Hepburn, Eleanor Roosevelt, or anyone else. They simply are interpretations meant to awaken you to a greater appreciation of the root triangle's existence—and its power. You'll probably find parallels to your own experience in these examples. They reveal a spectrum of three-way forces which no human being escapes and to which every human being has learned, productively or not, to adapt.

Ambivalent Intimacy: Katharine Hepburn

Katharine Hepburn's romantic involvements are common knowledge. She had one all-but-nonexistent marriage (she married briefly at the beginning of her career and almost immediately divorced). She later had a long-term affair with the deeply troubled Spencer Tracy—an affair that took place outside the Roman Catholic Tracy's marriage, and that made him feel guilty as well as fulfilled. Hepburn's romantic history reflects some early triangular dynamics and some deep-rooted conflicts about men.

One of Katharine Hepburn's root triangles runs as follows: (1) Katharine; (2) her mother, a well-known spokeswoman for women's rights; and (3) a grandmother who died before Katharine was born and who, in McGoldrick and Gerson's words, "elicited from her daughters a deathbed promise that they would all go to college."

Clearly, some of Katharine Hepburn's drive to "succeed" can be inferred from this root triangle: she was in a "line" of women whose legacy and expectations all but demanded "success." But Katharine had another root triangle—a tragic one—that reinforced more than just the drive to succeed. It also reinforced a separation from men. It consisted of (1) Katharine; (2) her brother, who committed suicide at the age of fifteen; and (3) Katharine's parents, who here can be taken here as as a single point of the triangle. Katharine felt pressure to "replace" her parents' son—to fulfill his promise as well as her own. The message she received to "achieve" was thus doubly given. But how did these root triangles affect her love relationships later on?

Katharine Hepburn's "female legacy," drawn from her maternal grandmother's side of the family, and the pressure she may have felt to replace her brother set her apart from men—made it all but mandatory that she compete with them, that she take up an almost embattled stance against them. Intimacy with a man could only be achieved "illicitly." The "apparent triangle" of Katharine, Spencer Tracy, and Tracy's wife kept certain barriers in place for Hepburn—barriers that, unconsciously, she may never really have wanted removed. Again, this is speculation, but even as speculation it illustrates some of the ways two different root triangles can merge to reinforce each other and profoundly affect all future attempts at intimacy.

Competing for Attention: The John Quincy Adamses

The root triangles that formed for John Quincy Adams's sons illuminate a very common triangle in which two parents who feel tension with each other attempt to resolve that tension by focusing on their children. Adams and his wife did so intensively with their children (at the expense of their marriage). The intensity manifested itself as negative with their eldest son, about whom they worried constantly, and who eventually committed suicide; and "positive" with their youngest son, whom they praised and encouraged with equal intensity, and who went on to become a successful statesman. This is not to suggest, especially, that the "successful" son was *happy*: only that he responded to his parents' attentions by "succeeding" in the outer world.

Each Adams son had, in effect, two root triangles. The stronger was (1) son; (2) accomplished but distant father who reinforced distance from son by focusing on tensions in his marriage; and (3) mother, whose real focus was likewise on her marriage's tensions, even if she (along with the father) *appeared* to show interest in her children. Children pick up instantly on whether they are receiving real, nurturing, unconditional love or not. Because the Adamses' sons did not sense that kind of love from their parents, they created a second, competitive root triangle: (1) parents (combined as a single force); (2) rivalrous brother; (3) rivalrous brother. Each brother may have exaggerated his respective "positive" or "negative" position in the family as a means of winning his parents' attention, the "successful" brother through his achievements, the "ne'er-do-well" through attempts at attracting his parents' sympathy (or even anger). It is at least plausible that each son's behavior was in large part a ploy to win parental attention neither son ever learned to acquire in any other way.

We can only speculate about the effects of these root triangles on later "love triangles," but from other people's similar experience I've seen, they almost certainly faced problems. It's common for someone who grew up with a root triangle like the Adamses' to choose a mate just as distant and self-absorbed as the parents were—and then spend the relationship attempting to get love and attention from that mate.

Sibling Rivalry: Eugene O'Neill

Unlike the John Quincy Adams family, Eugene O'Neill's parents, James and Mary Ellen, tended to *ignore* their sons due to the great tension they felt in their relationship. This may have led Eugene and his older brother, Jamie, to have an intense competitive relationship. They may have unconsciously wished that their conflict would distract their parents from their own tensions. Turning their fraternal relationship into a fierce rivalry would take their parents away from their war. Perhaps Eugene O'Neill's ambivalent feelings toward and difficult relationships with women in later life point out another common result of this kind of root triangle. His relationships with women were similar to his relationship to his brother, filled with ambivalence, hostility, and a desperate need to connect. The resentment the child feels against the emotionally neglectful parent almost always carries over and is acted out in later relationships.

Seeking the Powerful Partner: F. Scott Fitzgerald

F. Scott Fitzgerald had one of the most publicized, stormy, and ultimately tragic romantic relationships of the twentieth century: his marriage to the vibrant but deeply troubled Zelda, who eventually was institutionalized for insanity. How might Fitzgerald's root triangle have prepared him to choose Zelda?

Fitzgerald's root triangle consisted of (1) Fitzgerald; (2) a mother who attempted to "collude" with Fitzgerald against the father; and (3) the distant "outsider" father. Disappointed in her "weak" husband, Fitzgerald's mother focused on her son, creating a number of love-triangle dynamics Fitzgerald acted out later in life. Zelda was attractive to Scott Fitzgerald partly because she was such a strong, larger-than-life personality—reinforcing the sense Fitzgerald had from his mother of women as "powerful." When this backfired—when Zelda began to "fall apart," behave erratically, and become dependent—Scott Fitzgerald felt out of his depth. In a sense, he became his "weak" father, impotent to change or often even deal with his still powerful, but now frighteningly unreliable and alien wife. If he had not been trained to see his father as weak and therefore himself as ultimately a weak man, he may have found his own creative strength to help his wife when she turned from strong to weak. In a sense, Zelda "proved" to Scott Fitzgerald that he was his weak father's son as much as his adored mother's: all because of the root triangle into which he was born.

The Accommodator: Eleanor Roosevelt

It is now, of course, common knowledge that Franklin D. Roosevelt had a mistress during his marriage to Eleanor Roosevelt—a mistress in whose presence he died. That Eleanor accepted this arrangement, even if it caused her pain, seems consistent with her root-triangle background.

Eleanor Roosevelt's root triangle consisted of (1) Eleanor; (2) her father, an alcoholic whom she adored; and (3) a cool, distant mother, with whom she competed for her father's attention. It may be tempting to see her role in her root triangle as that of the "child of an alcoholic" (COA): children of alcoholics com-

monly feel the urge to subsume their own wants in deference
to others and to hope for love from people constitutionally incapable of giving it. Whatever effects are explainable through her
COA background, it's clear that the love triangles Eleanor
Roosevelt entered when she first married Franklin Delano
Roosevelt and later when FDR took a lover stemmed directly
from her root triangle. FDR's mother, Sara Delano, strongly
objected to his marrying Eleanor and competed with her for him
(reflecting Eleanor's root triangle precisely). When, later, FDR
became "weak" (reminding Eleanor of her weak alcoholic father)
because of his polio and turned to another woman for companionship, Eleanor must have felt tugged once again by those first
triangular dynamics. Again she played the role of "outsider" who
had to accommodate, accommodate, accommodate—a role she'd
been conditioned by her root triangle to expect and accept.

Lover vs. Spouse: The Kennedys

The Kennedys have a long history of having high expectations
of sons, and the effect this later had on their love triangles
appears unmistakable. For several generations (including two
before John and Robert Kennedy), numerous Kennedy men died
young or unexpectedly. Clearly, anyone who survived in the
Kennedy clan felt the burden of having, in a sense, to compensate for all those who did not. Root triangles might easily be seen
in the current generation of Kennedys, where the pattern has
generally been "strong" Kennedy, "accommodating" spouse, and
"Kennedy child" feeling the burden of the Kennedy legacy to
achieve in the wake of so many Kennedy deaths.

Part of this "achievement," at least for the male Kennedys, has
quite clearly had to do with sex. With so much pressure and
attention on Kennedy males, competition was fierce: each
Kennedy son felt the intense pressure to prove himself a man
not only in the world but in the bedroom. Joseph Kennedy's

affairs with women, including some Hollywood stars of the 1920s, with his wife Rose "stoically" bearing up, provided a potent root triangle. Jack, Robert, and Ted Kennedy's well-known womanizing mirrors their father's. As for the wives they married, Ethel and Jacqueline Kennedy continued the "accommodating spouse" tradition set by Rose Kennedy—"looking the other way," and devoting the bulk of their energies elsewhere. (Joan Kennedy, of course, was less accommodating, which may be why her marriage to Ted was destined to end.) Jacqueline, in particular, brought her own interesting triangle agenda to her marriage: she adored her own father, Jack Bouvier—who was an irresponsible, hard-drinking rogue and womanizer—and she may have created, in a sense, a Phantom Lover Triangle when she married: herself, Jack Kennedy, and her dead father. Her attraction to Jack Kennedy was almost certainly interwoven with her feelings about her father: the men's history as womanizers allied them in her mind, and getting the love of Jack may unconsciously have meant getting the love of her father.

The value of looking at these well-known people's probable root triangles and speculating about their effects isn't just to make some interesting historical gossip. I've chosen these examples because they begin to suggest the wide variety of patterns all of us have experienced in our root triangles. They give us, in fact, a list of concrete "lessons" that we've all learned in various ways and to various degrees from our root triangles. Let's take a look at the list again:

▲

LESSONS OUR ROOT TRIANGLES TEACH US

1. Ambivalent intimacy: the fear of letting go, allowing ourselves to be vulnerable in a one-to-one relationship.
2. Competition for attention: the anxiety that if we don't

bend over backward with attention-getting behavior, we can't get the love we crave.

3. Sibling rivalry: another variety of competition—the fear that we must "best" a sibling to get our share of love and attention.

4. Search for the powerful partner: looking to subsume ourselves in some larger-than-life person who can "fix" us.

5. Accommodation: becoming a doormat in relationships because we don't believe we deserve better.

6. Lover vs. spouse: separating sex from love, passion from nurturing, out of the belief that it's impossible to find both in one person.

These lessons go deep—and there are more we haven't covered here that we'll discover as we go along. But let's look more closely at one of the most common and damaging lessons many people learn from their root triangles, a lesson which lands them in any number of apparent triangles today—the one exemplified by the Kennedys: lover vs. spouse. Cultural stereotypes tell us that this split is mostly a man's problem; Jill's story is evidence that it is common for women, too. But her story won't only show how the split between sex and love can operate in a triangle—it will also hint at how that split can be healed.

▲

WHEN SEX IS OIL, AND LOVE IS WATER: JILL'S STORY

It wasn't easy for Jill—a quiet, gentle, attractive woman in her early forties—to make the confession she felt compelled to make in our first interview. "It's not like me," she said. "I wasn't brought up to live like this!" She lowered her head, rubbing her temples as if to erase an ache—an ache that obviously wasn't going away. She had told me about her husband, Richard—she had told me about her lover, Sam. "I'm a good mother," Jill continued. "I've always tried to be responsible, decent. Why did I let this happen?" Jill stopped massaging her brow and looked up at me. "And why can't I stop seeing Sam?"

Jill was far from a product of the sexual revolution. She had been born in a small midwestern town and brought up in a strict Lutheran household that had instilled in her a strong code of ethics and sense of morality and an unassailable belief in the "nuclear family." Jill was nothing if not conservative, and her pain at the split in her life right now was real and deep. "I can't understand why I let this happen," she kept saying. "I love my husband, but I seem to need Sam, too. It's tearing me apart."

The triangle in Jill's life was, to her, totally irrational. It had no basis in her past that she could see—it totally violated the fidelity she'd always believed marriage had to include. But when she met Sam—an attractive man recently hired by the insurance company where she worked—something went "nuts" in her. "It was as if I turned into someone totally different when I saw him," she said. "I've never felt that sudden an attraction before. I mean, I'd known my husband from childhood—we went out together in high school. My husband and I were like best friends. But Sam—" Jill shook her head. "It was like getting hit by a lightning bolt." Evidently the chemistry was mutual. "He tells me now that he *felt* how attracted I was to him from the first moment we met," Jill continued. "And he says I make him feel so desirable—he'd never met a woman before who made him feel this way."

Jill quickly discovered what she called a "Hyde" personality lurking beneath the benign "Jekyll" she'd always been before. She accepts full responsibility for initiating the affair. "I made up a reason I had to work late one evening when I knew Sam had to work late to get a project done, and I stood in front of the open door to his office when I knew everyone else had gone home." Sam turned around to see her, and smiled. "It was as if he could feel me standing there—feel my need for him." Jill still doesn't understand how she got the courage to walk up to him and reach out gently to touch his face, a touch that emboldened them to kiss. "It felt almost prearranged, somehow," Jill said, "like fate. It was as if we had no choice—we knew we had to be together somehow, some way. . . ." Jill's voice trailed off, and her face darkened.

"So we started going to—motels. Out of town. Using different names. Sounds like some bad B movie, doesn't it?" Jill paused again, then half angrily, half tearfully spat out: "I *hate* myself so much sometimes! I can't stand what this would do to Richard if he knew about it—to our kids—what it's already doing to my whole life."

Jill had kept her affair with Sam a secret from Richard, but she knew Richard sensed something was going on. "Even my kids know something's up," she said. "I know I get distracted—act more distant—when I come home after sneaking time with Sam. And I know my temper is short whenever Richard or my kids try to find out what's the matter." Jill stopped having sex with Richard, hating herself for it—she could sense how hurt he felt—but she just couldn't summon up any sexual passion for him anymore. Everything about Jill seemed to communicate "Hands Off!" Richard and she didn't feel equipped even to begin to talk about what was going on. Jill always had played the dutiful wife and mother and Richard the dutiful father and husband; they had each so strictly adhered to their expected roles that much of their shared life before now had been rote. They hadn't developed any real vocabulary to talk about their feelings because they were so used to burying any emotion they felt wasn't "appropriate."

"I knew I had to give Richard some explanation—and all I could think of was work. Sometimes I even rationalize to myself that that's what the problem is. After all, I did meet Sam at work! But I told Richard I had some difficult accounts, and that was why I was upset." Richard seemed to buy this for the moment, but Jill felt no less eaten up by guilt at her duplicity. "I hate myself for every lie. All I want to do when I lie to Richard is run out and find Sam—get out of the house and make love to him. That seems to be the solution to everything. But it's also the problem behind everything! All of which just makes me hate myself more."

Jill's pain stemmed not only from the untenable situation in which she felt she'd deposited herself, but from the powerlessness she felt over her feelings for Sam. Her triangle was compelling in a baffling way—she couldn't break the hold Sam seemed to have on her; neither did she want to destroy the settled, secure life she'd built with Richard. Her guilt told her that the "right thing" was to choose one man over the other, but she couldn't imagine how, or whom, to choose.

We've already seen that triangles don't come from nowhere— they're based on the building-block root triangle each of us knew when we were born, usually (although as we'll see later on, not always) you, your mother, and your father. I knew that to help Jill confront the issues in her "apparent" triangle, she'd have to confront some underlying issues attached to a triangle far more distant in time and place, although just as compelling now as it had ever been: the root triangle that she'd felt part of from infancy and to which she was responding unconsciously today. Take a look at what Jill and I found. It will serve as a useful introduction to the "root work" I'll ask you to do for yourself a little later on.

Even Roots Have Roots

At first Jill could see no connection between her current "other man" dilemma and anything in her past. (Remember her first words to me? "I wasn't brought up to live like this!") But eventually, she began to see that in a sense she'd virtually been *brought up* to react the way she did. She saw that her current predicament was intimately tied to her very earliest past.

"My parents were always so devoted to each other," Jill said when I asked her to tell me something about her childhood. "Mom adored Dad. Dad couldn't say a word without Mom beaming at him—and I was expected to follow suit." Jill smiled a little. "I guess we treated him a little like 'Saint Dad.' I don't remember my parents ever having a fight—at least not in front of me. In fact, you know how most people can't imagine their parents making love? Well, I can't imagine my parents fighting *or* making love."

Jill told me more about her family over the next several times she came to see me. It was clear to me that she "needed" to see her parents—and especially "Saint Dad"—as morally upright, beyond the pale, "better" than other people. Something else was clear. Both her parents had survived difficult, abusive childhoods—each had been brought up by angry, sullen adults. Jill's father was orphaned early and was grudgingly reared by distant relatives who had little money, less love, and no patience; neither he nor his wife, whose mother had died when she was a baby and whose distant, strict father dealt with her almost contemptuously, had ever felt "wanted." They were determined, said Jill, to produce a perfect home and a perfect family to make up for what neither of them had had.

As we'll see more clearly as we progress, the triangles we get into are affected by the triangles that have affected other people. In other words, our roots have roots. Our triangles and our parents' own root triangles influence each other and overlap. Jill's mother's root triangle made her attempt, unconsciously, to turn her husband into the parent who'd "abandoned" her by dying when she was a baby—while reflexively adhering to her father's strict moral standards in the (also unconscious) hope that she might win her father's love. Jill's father's root triangle caused him to demand attention and praise and devotion from his daughter and wife—the love he had never gotten from his own dead parents, at whom *he* was unconsciously angry because they'd "deserted" him.

Since both Jill's parents had been treated coldly, and sometimes cruelly, by the loveless people who brought them up, they both feared any violent or even passionate expression of emotion in their current lives. Each had learned that "anger" meant "I hate you," which meant each had learned that anger, and other "uncontrolled" emotions, were to be avoided at all costs. Consequently, their implicit message to Jill was that there was no such thing as a healthy expression of anger—or passion, or even unbridled *joy*. Emotions were dangerous, like lit matches over gasoline. You did everything you could to keep them under control, to repress them so that they wouldn't control you.

The toll this took on Jill (never mind her parents, who had grown up equally repressed) was enormous: she spent her whole life swallowing any "inappropriate" emotion (that is, anything her parents taught her was "angry" or "bad"), until that swallowed rage built up in her to the point where she couldn't stand it any longer.

The Bursting Point: How an Apparent Triangle Is Born

Jill virtually had to *create* a "Sam" to let out this bottled emotion. You'll recall at the beginning of this chapter what I said about the denial we often have about the role we play in "creating" a lover. We may desperately try to tell ourselves it's "fate" when we fall for a particular person, but this hides our readiness to "fall," and the unconscious *pursuit* we've made—we've often been searching all along, whether we know it or not, for our own versions of Sam.

Jill said that when she saw Sam for the first time she felt as if a lightning bolt had hit her. In fact, she had been a lightning rod aching for a thunderstorm for some time—Sam's "appearance" was something for which she had been unconsciously preparing herself for years! Jill experienced something like emotional spontaneous combustion. Her feelings had built up to such an unbearable point that they urgently sought release—not just any release, but a release "worthy" of them. Since she saw them as "bad" emotions, that meant Jill needed to do something "bad" to express them: have an "illicit" affair. Jill had a whole swallowed self aching for unbridled passionate, sexual expression—expression that, however, made her feel deeply guilty. It's no wonder this self found that expression in something Jill's parents would have found unspeakable: an affair.

The split I talked about earlier between the urge for sex and the urge to be nurtured is germane here: Jill's repressive root triangle had made this split particularly vivid in her and all but inevitable. Brought up not only to avoid rage or other "bad" emotions at all costs, Jill was also brought up to "adore" her father—to praise his every word and effort. Richard, because he was her husband, became the "acceptable" man in Jill's life—he took the psychic place of her father, and Jill revered him accordingly. However, this reverence was at odds with the "bad" sexual feelings to which she could never give complete expression in her marriage—feelings she had buried in herself. Feeling too sexually passionate with Richard would have been, unconsciously, almost incestuous—not too far from feeling sexual about her father, which was unthinkable.

The point is that Jill was in a dilemma in which the only recourse was a Sam. She needed to give unacceptable feelings an outlet, and quite rationally if unconsciously, she sought and found an unacceptable outlet: someone "illicit" with whom she could act out her repressed passion, could be Hyde instead of Jekyll. Sam, for reasons of his own, was only too willing to help this side of her come out.

This brings up another point that we've encountered briefly before and that will continue to crop up in every triangle we learn about in this book: complicity. You can be sure that Richard and Sam were operating from equally compelling root triangles of their own. (We'll explore similar complicitous arrangements later on in this book that will make it clear how they intermesh.) The point is, Jill hadn't set up her current triangle in isolation: she lived out a role in triangles set up by her lover and husband as much as they lived out roles in her arrangement. Again, *no triangle can be sustained without the complicity of its members*—even if (as is usually the case) this complicity is unconscious. Richard, although he didn't have "proof" of Jill's infidelity, was aware and, Jill knew, upset that "something was going on." However, when (much later) he came in with Jill for a couple's session, I saw that he was almost glad that Jill was "distracted" for whatever reason she was—even as he outwardly "worried" about her. Richard deeply sensed that Jill's passionate needs weren't being met by him, and he was afraid of those needs. He was secretly relieved that Jill had something else in her life to take the pressure off him—even as he *said* that he wished Jill wasn't acting so distant and upset.

Triangles "ask" to be sustained: each member has something crucial to express or achieve or escape from in a triangle. However, the deflection tactics sooner or later break down. And they break down more quickly when you awaken to your own complicity in maintaining them, as Jill is learning to do in therapy. It isn't that because she now understands Sam's "inevitability" she has magically lost all of her attraction to him. In fact, it's very common for the unconscious mind to resist even the most rational, plausible psychological explanation of behavior by provoking even stronger "negative" behavior. If Jill is deeply convinced she can only express the sexual, passionate part of herself via someone like Sam, it will take more than explanation to convince her otherwise. That terrified, inchoate, needy inner child—

that infant sensibility at the core of each of us—will let go of old reflexive assumptions only at its own pace, only when it feels secure enough to let go. All of us are conditioned subtly, pervasively, and deeply to believe we can survive only by adhering to certain behaviors. It takes more than intellectual argument to reroute a life.

But Jill's awakening is nonetheless a crucial first step. Already she has learned, first of all, that her urge to have an affair is not the monstrous, "immoral" atrocity she thought it was. Already she has begun to feel a glimmer of compassion for herself— merely by understanding that her behavior wasn't motivated by "evil." She now sees that it was the quite reasonable result of pent-up negative emotions that she had been taught throughout her life were inexpressible. That recognition, because of the recovery from the destructive effects of her triangular script it can make possible, is more than a beginning for Jill; it's a real triumph.

I've given you a lot of information here—I've touched on a number of concepts beyond the "split" theme with which I introduced Jill's story. We'll deal with all of these concepts, one by one, as we go on in this book. But for now, I'd like you to ask yourself some general questions about where your *own* root triangle(s) may have come from. As I've been promising, we'll get to a surprisingly simple method to determine and understand your root and apparent triangles in the program I'll set out in the next chapter. But now is the time to acquaint yourself with the broader canvas of your own past and your own immediate root triangle dynamics. What you learn in the following series of questions about your parents' effects on each other as well as on you should give you some valuable insight you'll be able to call on later, when you'll learn to make more specific connections to apparent triangles in your life today.

▲
LOOKING AT YOUR OWN ROOTS:
A QUESTIONNAIRE

Answer these questions in your journal.

First, consider your parents' relationship:

What was your parents' marriage like?

Who was the more dominant partner?

Was either parent particularly subservient to the other?

Did they argue a lot?

Did either one of them have affairs or flirt with other potential romantic partners?

Would you characterize their relationship as one filled with: understanding? repressed anger? distrust? disappointment? laughter? resentment?

Do you think they had lots of sex or only a little?

Did you feel theirs was a relationship you'd like to have with your partner?

Did you feel there was any room for you in their relationship?

Do you think you were ever "used" to help them distance themselves from each other—for example, asked to "take sides"?

Was there a lot of discord in the house? If so, how did that make you feel? Were you scared? Angry?

If there was discord, with whom did you usually side?

Now, take a look at your relationship with your mother:

Were you able to talk about serious things with your mother?

Did you feel judged or overly criticized?

Were you embarrassed by your mother?

Did you admire your mother? For what attributes?

Did you feel less "good" than your mother? For what reasons?

Do you think your mother admired you? Why?

Do you feel "just like your mother"?

In what ways are you sure she is quite different from you?

If you are a mother yourself, do you think you've improved on the job she did? How?

How does/did your mother feel she raised you compared with how she was brought up?

Now, take a look at your father:

Was there a lot of emotional or physical warmth between you?

Were you able to talk to your father about serious personal concerns?

What did you admire most about him?

Was there anything that scared you about your father?

Do you think you have anything in common with him?

Do you feel you've disappointed him in some way?

Did you feel you disappointed him in any way?

Did you feel admired by him? For what?

Did you feel he was too strict?

Did he make dating difficult for you? In what ways?

If you had a sibling:

Were either one of you labeled? ("The smart one," "the pretty one," "the talented one," etc.)

Were you very competitive in activities?

Did you feel like either parent's favorite? Why?

Did you think your sibling was either parent's favorite? Why?

Did you ever feel less good or much better than your sibling?

Do you have a memory of taking things out on your sibling?

Do you feel very guilty about things that happened between you and your sibling?

Do you hold yourself responsible for any of your sibling's problems?

Do you hold your sibling responsible for any of your problems?

If your sibling was the opposite sex, do you think that on some level you ever had a "crush" on him or her?

Simply by reading this far and making immediate connections, you probably have some new ideas about what your root triangles might be and how they've affected you. If insight hasn't already begun to develop, you're at least at the point of *readiness* for insight—a new look at who set you up for the triangular dynamics that grip you today.

Now it's time to start putting this readiness and whatever new ideas have already begun to occur to you to work. I promised you a step-by-step program to help you do this. The next chapter will map out that core program.

4

TRIANGLE AWARENESS AND RECOVERY

A TWO-PART PROGRAM

Y OU MAY ALREADY HAVE SOME STRONG CLUES ABOUT WHAT PEO- PLE OR "FORCES" CONSTITUTE your apparent triangle or triangles—or you may still be cloudy about exactly who's involved. Part of our task is to help you become clear about the members of your apparent triangle, and I'll help you do that in this chapter. However, once you've identified the three players in whatever three-way script you're in, you're only at the first step of triangle awareness. Simply knowing who the "culprits" are doesn't usually tell you much about why you allowed the relationship to form, what you're trying to get out of it, why it keeps you from growing, and—most important—how to escape it. You need to dig a little deeper.

Here's a basic rundown of the method I suggest to help you do this necessary digging—a method we'll be using with every triangle story we explore in this book. This "triangle awareness and recovery" method has two simple parts that add up to diagnosis and treatment.

Diagnosis means discovering your apparent and root triangles—and the "emotional triangle" that connects them.

Treatment means facing the fears and blocks that keep you attached to your triangle, and learning to resist "triangle triggers."

Let's take a closer look at each of these steps so that you can begin to understand how you can apply them in your own life.

▲
DIAGNOSIS

Every apparent triangle actually hides two others. One is the root triangle that we spent the last chapter exploring. The other is an *emotional* triangle that acts as a bridge between the apparent and root triangles. Discovering this "bridge triangle," the emotional triangle, means discovering what overriding feelings—what I call "feeling themes" and will explain more about in a moment—the members of your apparent triangle are living out.

Few people allow themselves to go beyond their surface likes and dislikes to realize that they've got these likes and dislikes for some very clear reasons. "I don't know why I love him; I just do!" or "Something about her makes my skin crawl; I can't help it!" is often as far as many people get about their feelings toward others. They don't realize that they are, in effect, "choosing" to feel one way or the other, positive or negative, about the people in their lives. They don't realize it because they're making choices based on some very early conditioning—which makes it appear that there's no "choice" at all: "That's just the way I am!"

In fact, there are a multitude of factors that lead to being "just the way" you are, and extricating yourself from destructive triangles depends on finding out what some of those factors are.

Let's illustrate how to do this with a common triangle scenario. We'll focus on a Lover Triangle, since it's easier to grasp than other triangle categories.

Jane has just found out that her husband, John, is having an affair with his secretary, Mary. Jane is devastated—especially because, although this is the first time she's actually "caught" John (she found a love note from Mary in his jacket pocket, which made their affair all too explicit), she's suspected him before. In his last job he often stayed late and went on spur-of-the-moment business trips that made her think he was cheating on her then, too.

Jane has no doubt that her husband has plunged her into a triangle. Asked to draw it and label its points, she does so with no hesitation:

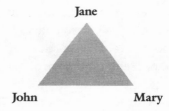

Jane

John   Mary

But now I'll ask Jane to go further. What are her feelings about each member of the triangle, herself included? I'll ask her not to analyze—just to put down the first descriptive words that come to her. She is able to come up quickly with the following three lists:

I feel that:

Jane is	John is	Mary is
angry	disloyal	seductive
lonely	cruel	dangerous
betrayed	insensitive	wily
powerless	selfish	powerful

Now I'll ask Jane to condense each of these lists of traits into three overriding summary descriptions—"feeling themes." Feeling themes are a set of emotions that we play out in our various roles as parent, child, lover, friend, etc. They sum up how we experience these roles at one point in time and how we experience others who are in roles important to us.

But coming up with catch-all feeling themes is difficult for Jane at first. So I offer some possibilities—possibilities taken from the stories you'll eventually read about in this book. I ask Jane if any of her feelings lists coalesce into any of the following common feeling themes.

Betrayer	Seducer	Disapprover
Intruder	Distant caretaker	Taskmaster
Victim	Fearful child	Joy-giver
Lonely child	Neglectful caretaker	Tormenter
Angry child	Smotherer	Bad child
Villain	Protector	Overachiever
Savior	Deserter	Underachiever
Accomplice	Guilty child	Needy child
Prisoner	Jailer	Jealous lover

I tell Jane she can come up with any feeling theme she'd like, whether or not it's on this list. She scans these columns, however, and realizes the following three themes she's found on them are exactly right:

Jane—Victim
John—Deserter
Mary—Seducer

Now I ask Jane to draw a new triangle next to her first triangle, labeling each point with a feeling theme rather than a name:

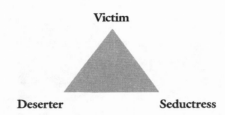

Victim

Deserter   **Seductress**

Now, quickly, I ask Jane to think who these themes most strongly bring to mind from her past, and to draw a third triangle, each point labeled with the name of the person that point's theme most vividly calls up for her. She's able to flash quickly on who two of the themes represent most strongly—she clearly sees herself as the victim in both her apparent and root triangles, and she immediately thinks of her father as the deserter. But who was the seducer?

It's generally the case that your root triangle's members will come to you quickly—simply by looking at and reflecting on each feeling theme, you usually have a strong picture of who it represents most strongly in your life. But sometimes, when you've spent years of your life denying that, for example, you are angry at a parent you feel you're supposed to love, a root presence can be blocked from your awareness. I ask Jane to flash on a vivid scene with herself as victim and her father as deserter. What was going on? Who was there? Who was doing the "seducing"? Jane has a sudden insight. She realizes that she'd always felt her mother was taking her father away from her. "Every time I'd capture his attention, like getting him to play ball with me in the backyard, my mother would always intrude and say he had to wash the car or go to the market—anything to get him from playing with me!" Jane, quite clearly, has found her "seducer."

Her root triangle now stacks up as follows:

Jane

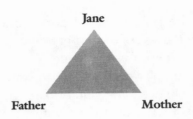

Father   Mother

Jane now realizes that her apparent triangle of John, Mary, and herself was just the beginning. She is astonished to realize that she is playing out a childhood role she'd learned with her father and mother. When I ask Jane to tell me about her father and mother, she describes feelings remarkably similar to those she's experiencing because of John's affair. Her mother demanded her father's attention all the time, and Jane, who adored her father, continually felt left out—deserted by him. Jane's husband's affair activated all these old familiar emotions; in fact, as she realizes when she thinks about it more deeply, she chose her husband because he was in many ways like her father: somewhat aloof, undemonstrative, a man she felt challenged to "make love" her.

Drawing three triangles the way Jane has just done is an amazingly effective way to let you see, first, the real feelings you have about yourself and the other members of your triangle and, second, to understand the source of those feelings. It's not that you always come up with the same feeling theme every time you look at the triangle: they can vary. As you'll discover in the triangle stories in this book, sometimes you feel like the victim in a triangle (when you feel "done wrong"); sometimes you feel like the villain (when you've initiated an affair that you feel guilty about).

So, as you can see, this three-triangle method is a quick way to get down not only to the root triangle behind the particular apparent triangle you happen to be in, but to explore the *feelings* that reflexively pop up when you're in the grip of a triangle. These feelings are your greatest guides—they signal that some-

thing needs to be looked at more closely and more dispassionately. Again, it's the task of the rest of this book to show you how
to look at those feelings as they come up, and to show how they
affect the way you play out the roles in your life (e.g., as lover,
spouse, friend, child, sibling, and/or parent). We're only setting
out the basics here. But what do you do once you've gained the
important knowledge of how your feelings, and your apparent
triangle, cause you to play the roles in your life as you do, and
how it all relates to your past? How do you begin to take steps
to get *out* of the triangle? We come to our second step.

▲

TREATMENT

There will always be times when you find yourself reacting fear-
fully, angrily, jealously, resentfully, or in any of the old ways your
triangulating self habitually reacts. But there are mental checks
you can employ to keep yourself from blindly following your old
paths. These checks are specifically geared to whatever type of
triangle you find yourself gravitating toward, and we'll learn
them as we go through upcoming chapters. But here are two
examples:

If you're in a Rotating Date Triangle (in which you go from
partner to partner to partner, usually juggling two at once),
when you feel the urge to "bolt" and find someone new, you can
learn to stop for a moment and ask yourself some hard questions:
How do I know this new person is so great? Will he or she really
be better than the last one? Is he or she as attractive as I thought,
or am I just reacting by reflex? Remind yourself of the difficulties
you've always had jumping into a new relationship without
thought. Affirm to yourself that you don't need to be validated
by "proving" your attractiveness—by getting whomever you've
fixed on to notice you. Remind yourself of the kind of *pleasure*
in a relationship you're only able to enjoy through patience—
giving yourself and a prospective partner time. In other words,

you can learn ways to *weather* the triangulating urge until you've regained clarity, stepped back, and kept yourself from jumping into a relationship careful reflection convinces you would be a mistake.

If you're in a Phantom Lover Triangle (in which the third presence isn't actually present but is perhaps a long-dead parent, or the memory of a first love), you can check your descent into old triangular tactics by reflecting on the "key scene" that keeps you grounded in that phantom connection, relive the scene, see it as clearly and dispassionately as you can, make specific note of what's different between that scene and the situation in your life today, and, finally, affirm that you have strength and resources, now, as an adult, that you didn't have in your key scene as a child. You can affirm that what's in the past is past, and that the present holds options and opportunities you can face in a new and freer way. This step-by-step process will prove to you that the past is over and doesn't have to intrude on your present.

These are only two ways of "treating" your triangle urge when you feel yourself about to succumb to old triangulating tactics. As I've said, you'll learn about these and many others in greater detail as we go on. And remember that since triangulators tend to get into more than one kind of triangle, it will be more than worthwhile to explore with me all of the ways you can learn to withstand the triangle urge, and the "triangle triggers" that bring the urge on—even in triangles you may think don't afflict you. You will probably discover that you're afflicted by many triangles you have no idea are part of your life now, so subtle are our attachments to them and so insidiously do triangles work in our lives.

But there's a third part to this program—a part that will take you beyond even the triangle-checking techniques you'll learn in every triangle category. Once you've allowed yourself to undergo all of this treatment, you'll find, organically, that you've reached a new point of self-acceptance. You'll have proved to yourself that

you can tolerate—and triumph over—old feelings of discomfort and fear that previously sent you headlong into a triangle. In the clarity this affords, you'll be able to connect—and you'll find that you *want* to connect—more deeply, warmly, and satisfyingly with your primary partner. Our last step is to take advantage of this new readiness for intimacy. The final goal of this book is to enable you to achieve the fullest, freest sense of intimacy of which you're capable.

To get to this final goal, we have to begin from where we are—which, at the moment, is at the doorway to an extraordinary range of triangle categories. Let's start our exploration with what is perhaps the most common (or at least the most visible) triangle of all, the Lover Triangle. You'll shortly see just how effective our diagnosis-and-treatment method is in dealing with the high drama of this triangle, and how effective the method can be when you employ it in the triangles in your own life.

5

THE LOVER
TRIANGLE

THE LOVER TRIANGLE IS THE
CLASSIC TRIANGLE—IT'S WHAT
MOST PEOPLE THINK OF WHEN
they hear the word "triangle." Standard feeling themes in the
Lover Triangle are ones you'll probably recognize: the "betrayer,"
who gets into an affair outside his or her primary relationship;
the "betrayed," who gets "cheated on"; and the "intruder," the
third outside lover who gets involved with the betrayer.

If you've ever been in a Lover Triangle, whether you felt like
the betrayer, the betrayed, or the intruder, you know how emotionally confusing it can be. Typical mood swings in the Lover
Triangle run from self-hatred and self-pity to rebellion and self-
righteousness. Each "player" in the triangle seems to you to
become larger than life—including you, whether you feel you're
the put-upon betrayed one or the deceitful villain. It's not hard
to see why Lover Triangles can be compelling. To put it bluntly,

they're pretty exciting stuff. Your emotions run at their peak. Passions loom large, drama is high. You feel like victims of fate. "I can't help it!" may be the straying lover's cry; "How could he do this to me?" the betrayed lover's lament; "I give him something *she* never could!" the intruding lover's defiant protest.

That, anyway, is one version of the classic scenario. But even if you haven't yet gotten into an obvious Lover Triangle, are you susceptible to one? Do you have the kind of triangulating personality that is likely to get you into this kind of threesome? Ask yourself the following questions and find out. Don't forget to record your answers in your journal. It is extremely enlightening to review your own thoughts at a future time. It helps you to discover if you indeed have changed—and grown.

▲
THE LOVER TRIANGLE QUIZ

1. Do you find yourself "blanking out" when you listen to your partner? Is it frequently difficult to pay attention to what he or she says?

2. Do you feel you've got a good relationship as long as you keep away from certain "charged" topics, like money, feelings, or sex?

3. Do you sometimes feel "absent" during sex with your partner, as if it's all happening to someone else?

4. Do you feel more comfortable when you're with your partner in other people's company than you do with your partner alone?

5. Do you often feel you can't depend on your partner for support or practical help?

6. Do you consistently find romantic fantasy more satisfying than your romantic reality?

You may see how some of these questions indicate a bent toward the Lover Triangle, but you're probably a little baffled by others.

others. Let's take a look at why answering yes to any of these questions signals a readiness to welcome a Lover Triangle. Be prepared for some surprises.

1. **Do** *you find yourself "blanking out" when you listen to your part-ner? Is it frequently difficult to pay attention to what he or she says?* Sometimes fear of intimacy or an unwillingness to grapple with certain issues your partner brings up causes a kind of spontaneous blackout. You shut off your receptors and don't really hear what your partner is saying to you. If you find yourself habitually "exiting" conversations with your partner in this way, it means you're actually trying to escape your *partner* on a regular basis: something about him or her threatens you. This frequently marks a readiness to accept the presence of a third lover—you either seek one yourself or tol-erate your partner's taking one. The "lover" becomes a kind of escape hatch, allowing you and your partner to escape one-to-one intimacy with each other.

2. **Do** *you feel you've got a good relationship as long as you keep away from certain "charged" topics, like money, feelings, or sex?* Habitually avoiding difficult topics, especially money, sex, and intimacy, keeps an obvious distance between you and your part-ner. While avoiding "charged" subjects may appear to keep the peace between you, it prevents you on a deeper level from allow-ing yourself to trust your partner, or to invite your partner to trust you. That lack of trust creates a kind of blank space—a space frequently taken up by a third presence with whom you or your partner feel you *can* "open up," a lover.

3. **Do** *you sometimes feel "absent" during sex with your partner, as if it's all happening to someone else?* We've already learned in this book about the very common split between sex and nurturing. Our conditioning often creates real obstacles to feeling sexually open and expressive with a partner. But when you bury this split—try to hide from yourself that you fear sexual intimacy—sometimes you unconsciously "turn off" and even feel disembodied when you're in a sexual encounter with a partner. This avoidance tactic often signals that you're ready to live out with someone else the sexual yearnings you've unconsciously decided can't be lived out with your partner. It may also send a message to your partner that it's all right for him or her to look elsewhere. All of which leads to a Lover Triangle.

4.   Do *you feel more comfortable when you're with your partner in other people's company than you do with your partner alone?*
Again, the fear of intimacy is a very common reason why we often withhold ourselves in a relationship—and an equally common reason we may gravitate to triangles. When you habitually find yourself surrounding you and your partner with other people by going out to party after party, club after club, eating in restaurants rather than staying at home, when you do everything you can to avoid being with each other alone, you're sending out a clear message that you *fear* being alone. You're in a state of almost constant readiness to "bolt"—as well as a state of readiness to admit the distraction of a lover.

5.   Do *you often feel you can't depend on your partner for support or practical help?*
Routinely "deciding" that your partner will be no help to you in a crisis frequently signals that you're ready for a Lover Triangle. If you feel your current partner is "always" unable to help you when you need it most, obviously you'll be open to someone else who *can* help. You may reinforce this pattern you've set up for yourself by choosing partners who promise to be inept or unhelpful. As illustrated in the story about Jill

in chapter 3, we often "create" the partners we unconsciously
feel we need.

**6. Do you consistently find romantic fantasy more satisfying than
your romantic reality?**
There's nothing wrong with fantasy. It can be a rich source of
pleasure. Romantic fantasy can, in fact, help to enhance your
relationship with your partner, not detract from it. When, however, you use fantasy to escape your partner—when it becomes
habitual—it can't help but detract from that primary relationship. It's often a small step from habitual fantasy to acting that
fantasy out with another "real" lover—which means you're setting yourself up, again, for a Lover Triangle.

As you can see from our explanations of the issues these questions bring up, the word "habitually" is the key. If you find yourself nodding a vigorous yes to one or more of these questions—if
they seem to hit the mark with you because you realize they're
what you "always" do or feel—you're probably on the road to
a Lover Triangle, if you haven't gotten there already.

Does it mean you're a "bad person" if you're susceptible to
Lover Triangles? Does it mean there's something "wrong" with
you if you can't find your mate more sexually or emotionally satisfying? As we've begun to see already and as you'll see much
more clearly as we explore triangles in this and other chapters,
blaming ourselves for triangulating is always unproductive. We
triangulate out of deep conditioning: on some level we're convinced we need our triangular escape hatches to survive. In fact,
all "blame" is unproductive in dealing with triangles—it pushes
away the real issues we need to face to confront and overcome
destructive triangular attachments. Learning to separate ourselves from the blame-mongering that Lover Triangles commonly engender isn't easy, but it's our main task. And it can be
accomplished, as you'll see.

It is always possible, of course, that the primary relationship you're in right now isn't the right relationship for you. Your urge to triangulate may spring from the quite legitimate feeling that your primary partner just isn't someone you want to be with. But that still doesn't warrant triangulating. Whatever motive you may feel in resorting to a Lover Triangle, it's still, at base, a desire to escape uncomfortable feelings you're afraid you can't survive by facing them head-on—and this attempt to escape usually has disastrous consequences.

▲

DENIAL AND BLAME-MONGERING

Love triangles—and particularly Lover Triangles—are heated arenas for denial and blame-mongering. "If only I were a better lover, younger, sexier, richer, smarter . . ." "If only she or he weren't so cold, distant, uninterested . . ." "If only he or she would get a divorce and marry *me* . . ." These are some of the common "accusations" directed at ourselves and others in Lover Triangles. Cultural conditioning can reinforce those reflexes to deny or blame (impulses triangulators already have in abundance!)—but all of this is simply a smoke screen. Blaming someone else means preventing yourself from gaining clarity about the real nature of your relationships and from understanding what it is you really want out of them.

The Lover Triangle stories you'll read about in this chapter will illuminate a lot of what really goes on in this kind of triangle. You'll discover that there is a much more effective way to talk about lover triangles than to accuse one or two of the participants of being at "fault," at least not in the accusative sense that "fault" usually suggests. It *is* a matter of responsibility—but we can't begin to appreciate that until we truly accept that we get into the triangle situations we do out of choice, albeit often unwitting choice—usually frightened, self-protective, and unconscious choice.

Solutions to destructive triangles don't always mean "Be a good person and go back to your spouse." Sometimes the desire to triangulate indicates that you're in the wrong primary relationship—but you're too frightened to muster up the courage to get out of it, so you "compromise" by taking on a lover. Triangles can camouflage any number of motivations and fears. But, again, we can't get anywhere until we begin to break through that camouflage so that we can see what's really going on.

Let's try to do that now with some common Lover Triangle situations, taken from the lives of women and men who come to me for help. The support they finally receive is help they learn to give themselves, no matter how helpless they originally felt in the relationship situation that initially propelled them into therapy.

▲

SECRET BETRAYALS: GRACE, DEREK, AND MARYANN

When Grace came to see me, she was three months pregnant and just beginning to show. Unfortunately, it did not seem to be a pregnancy that gave her much joy, as much as she said she desperately wanted another child. She had none of the glow you might expect from a happily expectant mother; her young, pretty face was instead prematurely lined with worry. It was hard for her to begin to tell me how she felt. She finally said that her husband, Derek, and she had struggled to have this child, their second. But even though they'd succeeded, she said Derek was ashamed that the "problem" had seemed to be his, because he'd always had a low sperm count. Although they had had one child already (Miranda, now seven years old and a "holy terror," Grace added with an exhausted sigh), they had tried for years to have another. "Derek wanted Miranda to have a sibling close in age so she'd have someone to play with, as Derek had with his own brother," Grace said. Although finally Grace had succeeded in becoming pregnant, Derek couldn't help feeling bitter because it had taken so long, because he wasn't somehow "virile" enough to have had it happen sooner. Derek was more distant from Grace than ever, and Grace was miserable. "I had so counted on feeling joy about this," she said, "and Derek's distance right now is tearing me apart."

It didn't seem to help her much to get this off her chest, however. There was something else—something she obviously felt was much more difficult, even impossible, to deal with. She finally came out with it: "I just found out Derek is having an affair." She said she felt devastated—alternately hurt and furious, self-blaming and accusatory. Derek was only thirty-seven—could it be an early midlife crisis? she asked me. How could he abandon her now, just when she needed him most? What had she done wrong? Or had she never really known him at all? Was he just a bastard she should simply divorce?

She knew the woman Derek was seeing—Maryann, a lawyer with whom Derek worked. "The quintessential New York career woman," Grace said—sophisticated, driven, no-nonsense, and very attractive, "the kind of woman who goes to a health club every morning at six, puts in a ten-hour day, and still looks fabulous at ten at night." How did she know Derek was having an affair with her? "She drove him home one night after Derek said he'd had to work late. They must have thought I was asleep, but I heard the car drive up and looked out the window—just in time to see them in a mad, long, passionate embrace. I can still feel the ice in my veins—I couldn't believe what I was seeing!" Grace didn't confront Derek that night. "I was too stunned," she said, "and somehow I couldn't believe it was really Derek's fault."

When I introduced Grace to the idea that she might be able to learn from actually *diagramming* the triangle she was in, she had no trouble coming up with her apparent triangle:

Grace

Derek   **Maryann**

Her feelings also spilled out when I asked her to complete the second stage of the diagnosis by listing how she felt about each triangle member, herself included.

I feel that:

Grace is	Derek is	Maryann is
hurt	heartless	conniving
angry	insensitive	callous
abandoned	neglectful	homewrecking
unattractive	unfair	cruel

Could she condense these feelings into "feeling themes"? It took some thought, but she managed to come up with the following emotional triangle:

Victim

Inadequate savior   **Cruel homewrecker**

Now, I asked her, whom did these roles most strongly bring to mind from her past? Grace struggled a bit with this. Her brow creased in a frown. It was as if she were trying desperately to keep herself from admitting something. I repeated the feeling themes she'd just written down: "Who was the inadequate savior, Grace? Who didn't help you when you needed help—who wasn't there when you wanted somebody to be there?" Grace's face turned from frustration to sorrow. "My father," she said quietly. "And who was the homewrecker—the person who made you feel so unsafe?" It was clear now; Grace no longer hesitated. "My mother." It had taken some evidently painful work, but she now had her root triangle:

As Grace amplified on why she'd come up with her final triangle, it was clear that her root triangle involving her parents had been abusive. Grace's father was an accountant who had left her mother when she was five; her mother had remarried an alcoholic bartender who was crude and abusive to both mother and daughter. During this time, Grace wasn't permitted to contact her natural father, who she said she used to dream might "save" her if she could ever get through to him. Derek, whom she met right after graduating from college, reminded Grace of the one picture of her father she'd managed to steal from her mother's private papers. She had clearly transferred her need for a savior to Derek, who, it turned out (for his own root-triangle reasons), was at first happy to oblige.

When, later, Derek came in with Grace for couples' counseling, I discovered that Derek's root triangle was in some ways similar to Grace's: he too had grown up without his natural father. His father had gone off into the army when Derek was an infant and had been killed in the war. The real force in Derek's life was his maternal grandmother—a strong matriarch who made all the decisions in the family and who ended up bringing up Derek herself. Derek felt stifled by this "grand old lady," as he called her: she was strict, cold, and Victorian.

Not having a father or any other consistent male role model had made Derek defensive about his maleness even before he discovered that his sperm count was low. It turned out he was sullen and withdrawn as a boy—he'd obviously felt a deep, buried anger at not having a father, at having to kowtow to his grandmother. When as an adult he had married Grace and learned about his fertility problem, it was as if his *virility* had been called into crucial question. He desperately sought validation of his manhood—his attractiveness as a man. Hence Maryann.

Turning to Maryann was for him a desperate act—he needed to prove to himself that he was virile, that he could attract someone as strong, competent, and attractive as Maryann. The reasons he *thought* he was having an affair ("Grace was spending so much time with "Meals on Wheels," with Miranda, with preparing for the new baby—she didn't have time for me anymore!") were, in fact, superficial. It's true that Grace's frantically busy life added to the distance Derek already felt, but the roots of his involvement in an affair ran much deeper.

Grace's feelings of being abandoned are less covert. Derek's affair simply activated all her old girlhood pain about not having a paternal caretaker who loved her, whom she could depend on. And yet, Grace also unconsciously felt—and felt guilty for feeling—that perhaps Derek *was* a bit less of a "man" than she'd hoped. Feeling shame at this, she crowded her life with activity partly because she didn't want to confront her own doubts and fears too directly.

What this means is that Grace and Derek *both* took flight from their marriage. However, when they began to realize that they were reacting on these unconscious levels, they began to see that many of the "betrayals" they were reacting to were imaginary or in the past. They were able to reconcile—and Derek was able to see that he didn't "need" Maryann to "prove" himself—

because they saw that they were really fighting old battles, battles that had nothing to do with them *right now.* They could begin to focus on anticipating the birth of a baby they really *both* wanted.

My clients teach me not to push them. Both Grace and Derek had to be ready to see what parts of their respective histories were negatively influencing their relationship—just as you need to be ready to understand what part of your past may be affecting your present life. However, you can move closer to that state of readiness about triangles when you accept this given: there are *always* deeper reasons for any triangle than appear on the surface. A triangle is like a volcanic island: we only see a small fraction of the mountain that forms it. The rest is buried beneath the sea—all the way down to the ocean floor. When you see a triangle, think of that island, and remind yourself that most of it is hidden from view. Accepting that can put you in a state of readiness to find out what's going on that you *can't* see.

There are a lot more surprises in store for you about what you can't see in a Lover Triangle. Not the least of them is discovering how many triangulators practice "polygamy." Are you a polygamist? Don't answer no too quickly—at least not until you've considered the following story about some polygamists who didn't think *they* were, either.

▲

LOVER TRIANGLE POLYGAMY: WHEN YOU CAN'T SAY GOODBYE

Strictly speaking, polygamy means having more than one spouse. But something similar, an emotional and sexual polygamy, often happens when people triangulate. What do I mean by "polygamy" in this context? Witness the Lover Triangles involving Sandy, Adam, Rose, and Sandy's family, and you'll see.

Sandy is thirty years old. She is an attractive brunette, but is painfully self-conscious. "I just can't seem to do anything right," she told me when she first came to see me. "It's as if when God passed out talent, he decided to experiment with me—see if someone could get along with no talent at all." Sandy had worked eleven years previously as a secretary, but the only thing she got out of that job was Adam, her lover—her *married* lover. "Adam was my boss. I guess there's a real difference in our ages—he's sixty now—but I never really noticed that. What I noticed is that Adam was the one man I'd ever met who didn't think I was incompetent. Adam gave me a chance—I loved him for that. But then he got into another business, and he couldn't take me with him. Not, anyway, as his secretary." What Adam proposed was something decidedly out-of-office. "He said he loved me," Sandy explains. "He wanted to be with me. He had this studio apartment near Wall Street that he used for out-of-town customers—he lived with his wife uptown—and he said we could meet there. So we did. I knew he was married—but he seemed to *need* me so much. I'd never felt needed or appreciated like that, not by any man. I've been with him—two or three times a week—ever since."

Sandy may not have felt "needed" by any other romantic interest until Adam, but she did get a lot of tension from other quarters. Her mother called her several times a day. "She's always worrying about me. I'm used to it now, but I wish she'd let up sometimes. I mean, I know she cares about me and all—but she makes me feel as if I can't do anything without her!" Sandy's father often visited her when he was in the city. "He's always bringing me take-out Chinese food or a box of candy, or giving me money," Sandy says. "He says he can't get a word in edgewise when Mom calls, so it's easier for him just to come in. Anyway, he wants to see for himself that I'm all right." Both parents smothered her with attention—making it clear by what they said and did that they didn't think Sandy was capable of doing anything without their help.

Actually, Sandy had made some attempts to upgrade her job after Adam left, but she's never felt she had much to offer, so she gave up after the first turn-down. "I'm just no good at anything, anyway," she said. "Adam's thinking I was so terrific was a fluke. I'm sure he kept me on because he liked me, not because I did the job well." Sandy has become almost a recluse. She rarely strays from her apartment except to go to work or walk two blocks to Adam's apartment to see him when he's downtown.

It was Sandy's depression about her own withdrawal that brought her to me. However, I quickly saw that she'd benefit from attempting to diagnose what was going on in her triangle. At my suggestion, she mapped out the following as her apparent triangle:

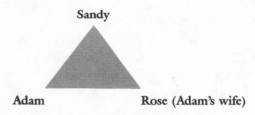

Her feelings list about each triangle member as follows:

I feel that:

Sandy is	Adam is	Rose is
needy	protective	intrusive
unprotected	understanding	nagging
frightened	loving	unloving
insecure	patient	self-absorbed

How did these feelings translate into feeling themes? Sandy hesitated. "I'm not sure," she said. I asked her to picture when she felt the most needy, unprotected, frightened, and insecure in her life. How would she have described the little girl she saw? She began to mouth "helpless"—then, with more authority: "I felt like a helpless child." Once she was able to articulate her own feeling theme, the other two became clear to her by contrast. Her emotional triangle emerged as follows:

Helpless child

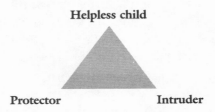

Protector   **Intruder**

And whom did these three feeling themes bring to mind most strongly from Sandy's past? Sandy hesitated again, and then asked herself some questions, whispering aloud to herself: "Who was always barging in? Who was always messing things up?" After a moment, she all but said "Aha!" and wrote down a name. "And who protected me?" This came more quickly. Her root triangle was now clear to her:

Sandy

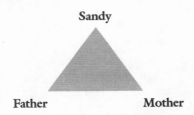

Father   **Mother**

As Sandy talked more about the smothering connection she had to her parents, it was increasingly clear to me why she'd come up with her root triangle and why it affected her so strongly.

Sandy's mother dominated her life. It was significant that Sandy's father said he could never "get a word in edgewise" and that he visited Sandy in the city almost as if he were a lover sneaking away from his wife. Sandy experienced a rivalrous Oedipal conflict: because her father could not save her from her mother's clutches, she retaliated by taking some other woman's husband— Adam. Because she got such a strong message from her parents (and especially her mother) that she didn't have the resources to survive on her own, Sandy longed for that "absent" caretaker with even greater intensity. In fact, *one* caretaker could never be enough: she had to surround herself with as many as possible.

Sandy was, in fact, resorting to a kind of polygamy. She was, in a sense, "married" to Adam, who was also married to Rose, but all these caretakers weren't enough to assuage her fears. Her withdrawal and introversion were intensifying, despite all the measures she'd unconsciously taken to protect herself. Sandy's mother was unconsciously comfortable with Sandy's having an affair with a married man that wasn't leading to marriage—and even with Sandy's being a homebody—because it meant she never fully had to give Sandy up to a man or a job. She could remain "married" to Sandy as well as to her husband. Adam kept his affair with Sandy and his marriage going for a number of reasons: having a younger lover made him feel he was holding on to his youth, kept him from facing full intimacy with his wife, and distracted him from the unpleasant realities of his job.

In fact, all members of these triangles are practicing a kind of polygamy: they have arranged their lives so that they're "married" to as many people as they need to ease the tension in their lives. But, especially for Sandy and Adam, these multiple marriages aren't working out. The "rewards" of avoiding responsibility for their own lives are crumbling, and they're both miserable.

Saying Goodbye

In the kind of polygamy we see in Adam, Adam's wife, Sandy, and Sandy's parents, no one ever has to separate completely from the childhood family. No one is forced to go through the pain of saying goodbye. This, I knew, was the real problem for Sandy and Adam: they were using their affair to hold on to and reinforce old messages about themselves.

Sandy was reinforcing her "inferior," subordinate status by

having an affair with a man who was already taken by another woman. She also reinforced this by taking refuge in being thought incompetent: by expressing abnormal needs, she could force the caretakers in her life to pay more attention to her. But having an affair with Adam was also getting back at her dominating mother who had crowded out her father: Sandy retaliated by taking another married man away from his wife. As for Adam, turning to Sandy (who was twenty-four years younger than he) was, first of all, an attempt to avoid the fact that he was getting older. Sandy's dependence made him feel powerful: he could take care of her as well as his wife, and for a while this compensated for the increasing lack of power he felt at work. Keeping a lover in the city away from his wife also gave him the feeling that he was keeping "options" open—that his life wasn't coming to an end.

Learning to "say goodbye" is essential. Sometimes we hold on to old hurts and unresolved problems from long ago so obsessively and unconsciously that we experience devastating effects in our current lives. We can't help but impede our own growth—we can't help but move backward—because, in a sense, we're trapped by the past. The task is to find out what is trapping us, to discover what's beneath what *seems* to be the problem in our lives today.

Once Sandy faced up to the old hurts she felt about being smothered by her mother and not "saved" completely enough by her father, pieces of the puzzle began to fall into place. She began to see that she was projecting onto Adam and her parents her own anger and despair. This freed her in other ways: slowly, she didn't feel as "needy" as she had felt before, now that she was facing up to what the anger and frustration she felt was really about—now that she was calling it by its real name. This had a curious effect. She could no longer quite mythologize Adam and her parents into the larger-than-life caretakers she'd seen them as before. She began to realize that she had, in a sense, *created* them. Because she felt she needed to be taken care of, she had tried to turn them into the caretakers she "needed." She was, slowly, learning to "say goodbye" to the old Sandy—and to her parents. She gradually accepted that her parents were (and would always be) central to her childhood but didn't have to be central to her life as an adult. She was beginning to "say hello" to Sandy as she really was today—and to the Sandy she could be.

Sandy's work in therapy has had other dividends. Now that she's feeling less needy, she's unwittingly encouraging Adam and her parents to face up to the ways they're trapping themselves. Since Sandy is learning not to react in the old "needy" ways and therefore is not playing the triangle game the way Adam and her parents had been used to, Adam and her parents are having to reexamine their own roles in Sandy's life. They're being nudged into new awarenesses, and are moving closer to saying goodbye to old messages to which they've been reacting reflexively in their own lives.

This process of learning to say goodbye isn't easy. It requires you to do two things: find out what the old messages are that are holding you back; and reassure yourself that you can survive *without* those messages.

Learning to do this is a trial-and-error process, and it takes time and patience. You'll learn in the "Diagnosis" and "Maintenance" sections coming up in this chapter, and throughout the rest of the book, how to begin this process in some concrete ways. And one of the most important lessons you'll learn is simply this: you can give yourself permission to disagree with any parental yeses and nos which are clearly holding you back. You do have the power to separate yourself from this conditioning; you *can* say goodbye to messages that are no longer helpful, that no longer really tell you what you want to hear, that don't help you to grow.

Not everyone who gets into a Lover Triangle in response to "old messages" gets out of the triangle. Some people may live in triangular dynamics throughout their lives. But they always pay a price. A person's adaptation to a triangle is a little like a plant's trying to grow through concrete: it may make it through, but it will be contorted, and it won't grow to full size. Witness the following story about a years-long triangle, a triangle which, although it had its compensations, exacted a toll on all three members that none of them can quite measure.

▲

SETTLING FOR LESS: THE UNEASY TRIANGLE THAT LASTS

Albert and Charlotte have been married for fifteen years. Born in England, they share not only a common culture, but an English reserve. It turned out that that "reserve" was hiding a great deal of emotion—emotion Albert and Charlotte have never quite been able to allow themselves to face.

Albert is a doctor, and passionate about his work: Charlotte says he lives for his patients. "I feel, sometimes," Charlotte told me, "as if I'm living not only with Albert, but with several dozen cancer, heart, and lung patients—he brings me through every detail." Childless, Albert acted as if his patients were his children. Charlotte, however, seemed to have made her peace with the intrusion of Albert's work: "Why would I want to take that away from him? It's what he lives for." It was clear, however, that Charlotte hadn't completely put up with her husband's inattention. "I don't depend on Albert for *everything*." She smiled. "There *is* Patrick."

Patrick is a research biologist who works at the same hospital as Albert, and Charlotte says he and Albert have been friends—best friends—for years. "Albert is always saying how brilliant Patrick is—but Patrick never takes himself quite so seriously," Charlotte said, smiling again. "Frankly, he's a refreshing antidote to Albert, sometimes."

Charlotte and Patrick were having an affair—in fact, had been having one for over ten years. Did Albert know about it?

"Nothing's ever been said outright," Charlotte explained, "but I suppose Albert might have a clue. I mean, it's hard to tell, since he's always so bound up in his work. But sometimes—I don't know—I think Albert is actually glad that I seem to be 'taken care of' elsewhere." Was Patrick content with this arrangement? I wondered. "Oh, Patrick is the perennial bachelor," Charlotte said a little wistfully. "I can't imagine him ever getting married. No, our early evenings together—our brief afternoons at his flat when Albert is away at work—they're really enough. Enough for him—and for me." Charlotte sighed a little. It seemed clear that while this "compromise" was holding up well enough, it had drained something out of her. Why, anyway, had she come to see me for help?

Charlotte said she'd come because she couldn't seem to fight off her periods of "blues" as easily as she once could, and she was wondering, most of all, if I might be able to suggest some medication that would help. She said she wasn't ready to do the kind of "delving into things" she knew "therapy" was all about—it was just that, well, her depressions were happening more and more frequently and they were beginning to frighten her. She was sure it was nothing all that important, and yet . . .

When I explained a bit about my "triangle diagnosis" techniques, Charlotte was relieved: "I can find all this out simply from a few diagrams and lists?" I told her that was the *beginning*, anyway. She came up with the following, starting with her clear apparent triangle:

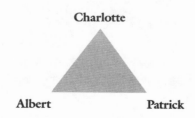

Charlotte

Albert   **Patrick**

Her feelings lists ran as follows:

I feel that:

Charlotte is:	Albert is	Patrick is
private	forgiving but distant	amenable
controlled	frightened of intimacy	comfortable sexually
depressed	unemotional	undemanding
needy	self-absorbed	kind

What feeling themes did these feelings call up? Charlotte ran her finger down each list and thought for a few long moments. She finally came up with the following emotional triangle:

Neglected child

Absent caretaker   **Distant caretaker**

And the root triangle her emotional triangle called up most strongly? Looking at the characterizations she'd just written down seemed to give her a revelation. She wrote:

Charlotte

Father   **Mother**

Charlotte's root triangle became clear as she told me more about her upbringing. She had been born into an academic family at Oxford. Her father was a fairly distinguished professor of history, her mother an art historian. "I suppose I had a privileged childhood," Charlotte said. "Not that it was especially luxurious. Oxford dons don't live all that well. But we didn't lack for conversation—for a good deal of 'culture.' The house was always full of people hotly debating this or that abstruse point. I remember, as a child, wondering what they were all talking about—wondering if I might ever grow up to use such big words." Charlotte said in passing that although she was an only child, all those adults didn't pay much attention to her. "No one quite knew what to *do* with a child—someone with whom you couldn't discuss Hegel was quite out of their league," Charlotte laughed. But the laugh was a little bitter.

The more Charlotte described her mother and father, the clearer it was to me that she had almost exactly matched them emotionally with Albert and Patrick. Her father was "totally absorbed" in his work, just as Albert was now. Her mother took a slightly lighter view of things—she was more "available" than her husband—but she still kept up clear boundaries. "I remember once coming home from school with an essay I'd written that my teacher had really liked—I guess I must have been about ten years old. Anyway, I burst into my mother's room with the essay, screaming, 'Mummy, Mummy, look what the teacher said!' I'll never forget my mother's reaction. She'd been sitting at her desk, her back toward me, and she turned slowly around. 'Darling,' she said, 'you should never burst into someone's room like that. People have a right to their privacy.' As you can imagine, the only way of pleasing my parents at that time was through 'academics,' and I had really hoped that my mother would be as happy as I was that I'd succeeded. . . ." Charlotte paused, then sighed with resignation. "But none of that really matters, does it? I mean, my mother was perfectly kind to me. She just wasn't especially—*emotional,* I suppose." Neither, it turned out, was Patrick.

"I feel comfortable with Patrick," Charlotte said, "because he seems to know when to leave me alone. He's kind and understanding and funny—but he's never tried to force his moods on me. He's the most accommodating man I know."

Patrick performed, it seemed, two functions for Charlotte: he gave her attention, but never went overboard with anything resembling a wild protestation of love ("I can't stand emotionalism," Charlotte said more than once); and he also allowed Charlotte to play her *mother's* role with him. With Patrick, *Charlotte* could call the shots: she could be who her mother was when she turned to that little girl so many years ago and kindly but firmly explained that you should never burst into someone's room. Charlotte had accomplished two things with Patrick: she'd found someone who was as emotionally distant as her mother, but also someone whom she could treat as her mother had treated her. And Albert, of course, simply "went about his business," as distant a background figure as Charlotte's father.

Even though, through her triangle diagrams, Charlotte realized the connection between her root triangle and the triangle in her life today, I knew she needed to see it more than intellectually. She had to acknowledge the *pain* she'd felt as a little girl, shut out by so many grown-ups—she had to acknowledge that the pain had made her needy even today. But these were messy feelings to Charlotte—they frightened her too much for her to really embrace them. It's no wonder she resists going deeper. She continues to cling to her Lover Triangle because it is so carefully and effectively constructed to keep her from feeling what she's terrified to confront: the needy little girl still locked up inside her.

Is there a problem with this? Should we always "deconstruct" our triangles, even if they're "working"?

The problem with most triangles is that even when they "work," they work in essentially limited ways. As we saw with Sandy and Adam, and earlier with Grace and Derek, *we take flight from ourselves* in triangles: they keep us not only from exploring the truth about our feelings, but from making free, fearless choices. Triangles lock us not only into certain rigid relationships, but into a constricted and fearful sense of ourselves. Eventually, Charlotte's "needy little girl" will have to come out—at least if Charlotte is to have any hope of finding real satisfaction in her emotional life. She can't remain content and continue to deny the existence of her deepest feelings and needs. It is true that some people go through their entire lives without fully acknowledging their deepest needs—but they can become very bitter, unhappy, even vengeful people. The refuge of the triangle may turn into a cage, a terrible cage that keeps you from living openly, freely, or with any kind of true contentment.

We can see something else in Charlotte's story. At the basis of her apparent triangle (involving Albert, Patrick, and herself)— and in fact at the basis of *every* triangle—is an unresolved tension between "significant" family members which makes it impossible for them to truly, psychically *release* each other. (We saw this perhaps most obviously in Sandy's mother, who was unconsciously willing to encourage her daughter's isolation and affair with a married man because it meant she wouldn't "lose" her.) It's as if we are addicted to the "unfinished plots" in our lives—we are drawn to them again and again, desperate to play them out until we *have* in fact "finished" them.

This impulse gets us into trouble when it leads to triangles, which merely recreate (as well as reinforce the effects of) the old dramas and keep us just as stuck as we ever were in our "unresolved plots." But the impulse to "finish" the plot can also be a productive one. We do, in fact, need to come to closure about unresolved problems in the past. The problem is that we can't achieve true closure by "acting out" our pasts over and over (much as our unconscious minds tell us we can). The only way to achieve closure is through understanding and then acceptance of what really went on in the past, what you may have felt then, and how that past is affecting you today. (We'll explore this in greater detail in chapter 7, about Members of the Family Triangles.)

The Lover Triangle—with its high drama and heady emotions—is a very effective tool to keep you stuck: it can allow you to replay your old scripts over and over while convincing you that you're actually in "new" relationships. Your own highly charged feelings blind you to the fact that you're simply beating the same old dead horse. But if the way out of the Lover Triangle trap is through understanding and acceptance, we need to increase our ability to gain insight into the private world of our feelings—we need to dig beneath our "apparent" problems to the dilemmas that are really motivating us.

You can't get to acceptance before you've achieved awareness, which is something you've already begun to do by answering the questions you've been invited to ask about yourself in these chapters. Focus on our next "Diagnosis," "Treatment," and "Maintenance" sections to see how you can start to achieve awareness and acceptance—and begin to break through the denial and blame-mongering that Lover Triangles so often lock us into.

▲

DIAGNOSIS: DIAGRAMMING YOUR OWN INVOLVEMENT IN LOVER TRIANGLES

If you're *in* a Lover Triangle, either as victim or as perpetrator, you probably know it. But take some time to diagram what you know in the ways I've outlined. First, draw your apparent triangle:

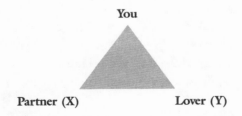

You

Partner (X)   Lover (Y)

Now, quickly, without analyzing, list your feelings about each member—how *you* feel, and how you feel about whoever you've labeled X and Y:

I feel that:
I am   **X is**   **Y is**

Take a moment to register each list of feelings. Can you condense them into feeling themes? If you need help, go back to chapter 4 and the list of possible Emotional Triangle feeling themes. Come up with your own themes if these don't apply— label them in whatever way seems to sum up each triangle member's net effect most powerfully for *you*.

Now draw your emotional triangle. For example:

Victim

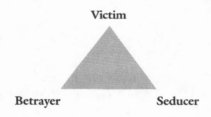

Betrayer   **Seducer**

Just as quickly, reflect on who each feeling theme most strongly brings to mind from your past, and draw your root triangle. If one or more presences in the root triangle don't come easily, reflect on the role or roles that do come easily. Let yourself *feel* your own feeling theme as vividly as possible. Note who is in the scene with you—does he, she, or they fill the feeling themes you're seeking to fill? As I said when we talked about this process in chapter 4, you generally won't have a problem flashing on who originally or most strongly played the roles in your root triangle. But if you do, allow yourself to visualize your way to an answer.

You may come up with the classic parental root triangle, like the following:

You

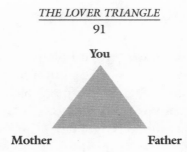

Mother   Father

The value of finding your root triangle is enormous. You may discover that simply being able to label who taught you to play the triangular roles you've learned to play can be cathartic: you may see immediately that you *don't have to repeat them today.* At the very least, you'll have an "Aha!" moment that I promise you will eventually help you to separate appropriate responses from inappropriate responses in your relationships today.

▲
TREATMENT: HEALING THE SPLIT

Perhaps the most difficult task people who continually get into Lover Triangles face is reconciling their need for nurturing with their desire for romance or sex. Even if you don't feel as neat a split as this, if you get involved in a Lover Triangle, you still experience a divided self—divided between what you're convinced one person can't give you and what you perceive only another person can.

Checking the urge to enter a Lover Triangle means asking yourself some questions you may never have allowed yourself to consider about this "split" dilemma. First of all, you need to find out what it is you're truly after.

You may think you know. "Good sex." "Understanding." "A shoulder to cry on." However, your needs are rarely as simple as this. It is perfectly appropriate to desire sex, understanding, and sympathy in a love relationship, but for habitual Lover Triangulators, the desire often masks deeper needs and fears that aren't being addressed.

When the desire for whatever it is you're convinced you can only get from someone outside your primary relationship becomes particularly acute, take a moment to examine what you're feeling. Open up your journal and ask yourself:

▲ What are my emotions right now? Am I feeling trapped? hurt? lonely? angry? bored? resentful? depressed?

When you've isolated the feeling or feelings that come up most strongly, you've found something very important: a "triangle trigger." A simple feeling or mood can be all a triangulator needs to act out his or her urge to connect "elsewhere." Before you give in to that urge, take the time to reflect on whatever emotion is strongest, and ask yourself, first:

▲ What do I really want right now?

Let's say you come up with the following list:

> A lover
> Sex
> Fun

Examine each of these desires in turn, as follows:

▲ Do I really want another lover—or do I want more understanding?

▲ Am I really after sex—or do I long for closeness?

▲ Do I want to have fun—or do I just want to escape the feeling I'm having?

If, when you're honest with yourself, you realize that you're after something deeper and more general than you first thought you were ("understanding" more than the mere companionship of someone else; "closeness" rather than sex with the particular lover you've been fantasizing about; "escape" rather than fun), that's fine. Affirm that you're *entitled* to what you want. But now ask yourself if you've got alternatives:

▲ Can I turn to my primary partner for the closeness, escape from pain, and understanding I'm after?

▲ Have I attempted to be emotionally close with my part-ner, or invited him to be close to me?

▲ What might happen if I did?

Answer this question as honestly as you can. Visualize approaching your partner, allowing him or her into your life, your heart and mind—visualize becoming receptive to your partner. Make this visualization as specific a scene as possible. Perhaps you'll see yourself walking with your partner, hand in hand, on a beach on a summer night; perhaps you're both in the warmth of your bedroom, under a quilt; or perhaps at a favorite intimate restaurant, just the two of you and the candlelight. Imagine yourself getting what you need from the partner you're with. Experience all the detail of this scene and the feelings it brings up as vividly as you can.

What you're doing is opening a door—allowing for the pos-sibility that the closeness you crave might be possible to achieve with your partner. Healing the split often means having the cour-age to imagine that you are capable of getting more from your primary partner than you've allowed yourself to see. Whenever your triangule trigger comes up, these questions and visualiza-tion techniques can go a long way toward convincing you that your partner may have more resources than you know. Once you start to accept that, it's all but certain that Lover Triangles won't have the appeal they once did.

6

THE PHANTOM LOVER TRIANGLE

THE PHANTOM LOVER TRIANGLE IS ONE OF THE MOST PERPLEX- ING. IF YOU'RE IN ONE, YOU probably don't realize that there *is* a "third presence" influencing your behavior in your primary relationship. And even if you do become aware that you're trapped in a Phantom Lover Triangle, getting out of it—inviting the "phantom" to leave—can seem all but impossible. We cling perhaps more fiercely to our phantoms than to anything else.

What are some examples of the third—phantom—presence that creates a Phantom Lover Triangle?

It might be the internalized "voice" of your mother or father (whether they're now dead or alive); it might be an ex-lover you haven't really gotten over (as much as you may not be "aware" of him or her at the moment); it's often a "first love" from long ago to whom you can't help comparing whomever you're with today. Whoever ends up influencing you, however, creates a powerful voice—and usually a very destructive unconscious obstacle—in your love life.

If Phantom Lover Triangles are so unconscious, how is it possible to detect them? I've come up with a quiz to help you determine whether or not this is your favored method of triangulating. Answer yes to one of more of the following questions, and I guarantee that a ghost has moved into your love life—and is probably wreaking a fair amount of havoc. Take the time to put the answers in your journal before you turn the page.

▲

THE PHANTOM LOVER TRIANGLE QUIZ

1. Do you idealize your parents, or, conversely, do you vilify them and feel ashamed of them?

2. Is it hard for you to imagine your parents having sex?

3. Do you feel "caught" by a past love affair—do you go over and over certain past relationships in your mind?

4. Do you find yourself constantly comparing yourself to other people, or do you compare your lover to other people?

5. Do you feel you are incapable of being a "grown-up" in your relationships—do you feel that other people always seem to know the "adult thing" to do, but you never do?

6. Do you find yourself getting depressed at a particular time every year, but you don't know why?

Some of these questions may seem baffling, which is not surprising, since they probe often baffling triangles. Let's take a moment to go over why I've chosen these questions and why answering yes to them means you've got a ghost in your love life.

1. *Do you idealize your parents, or, conversely, do you vilify them and feel ashamed of them?*
In chapter 2 we investigated the triangulator-predictor question

"Do you think of any member of your family as a complete 'nothing'?" When we mythologize our parents into ogres or saints, we set up the need for a third presence to "compensate" for them if they're ogres, or live up to them if they're saints. In Phantom Lover Triangles, one or both of these idealized or shameful parents can become a phantom presence— mythologized "superpowers" that you've allowed to live deep in your unconscious mind and that can interfere with any relationship you get into today.

2. Is it hard for you to imagine your parents having sex?

It is very common for people to shy away from the idea of their parents' having sex, or *enjoying* having it. Because of the puritanical way most of us have been brought up to think of sex and some very strong Oedipal issues that may make it threatening, on a psychic level, to imagine our parents making love, the very notion is often anywhere from distasteful to unthinkable. I hold it as an axiom, however, that unless you can imagine your parents enjoying sex with each other, you're blocked in some crucial ways from fully enjoying sex in your own life. Why? Because when we accept that our parents are capable of sexual feelings—and capable of enjoying them—we humanize them; we relate to them not as overweening "superpowers" but as people who are as vulnerable and "real" as we are. We are then free—free of their "voices"—to express ourselves in love as we choose.

Few of us don't have some difficulty with this, however, which means that most of us, in some ways, are prone to Phantom Lover Triangles—in which the phantom is an internalized sexual taboo in the form of your father or mother (or both parents together as a single force) saying "No!" When that voice is particularly powerful, it can lead to some profoundly uncomfortable Phantom Lover Triangles—triangles that prevent you from expressing yourself freely as a sexual, loving person.

3. Do *you feel "caught" by a past love affair—do you go over and over certain past relationships in your mind?*
This is a more obviously leading question. When you're obsessed by a past lover, that lover clearly becomes a phantom who you may be all too aware is crowding the primary relationship you're "really" in today. But sometimes that phantom presence can be very subtle. As you'll see when we discuss "cutoffs" a little later, we often push ex-lovers with whom we haven't come to emotional closure down into our unconscious, where they continue to play a very active role in our love lives. They can keep us stuck in unconscious reactions to our current partners, stuck in certain unproductive assumptions about relationships—assumptions we can't change until we become aware that a phantom lover is making us hold on to them.

4. Do *you find yourself constantly comparing yourself to other people, or do you compare your lover to other people?*
This is a variation on our third question. If you consistently compare yourself or your partner to others, those others are playing a very active phantom role in your life. Sometimes this can turn into a "rotating phantom" triangle—in which, because you don't feel secure about yourself or about your partner, you can't *help* but see yourself or your partner in comparison to almost anyone else you meet: neither of you has enough "reality" to stand on your own. As I've already intimated, the root of this Phantom Lover Triangle is intense self-doubt—the disbelief that you and your partner are sufficient just as you are.

5. Do *you feel you are incapable of being a "grown-up" in your relationships—do you feel that other people always seem to know the right thing to do, but you never do?*
This, again, has to do with a deep feeling of self-doubt. You are virtually pleading for a third presence to come in and "save" you when you don't feel you're adequate in a relationship. In fact, I

guarantee that if you're in a relationship and you feel you're not "enough," you've already got that third presence within you—an internalized negative voice that keeps *telling* you you're not "enough." The other people who always seem to know the right thing to do are in fact stand-ins for this internalized presence— perhaps an ex-lover who treated you like a child; perhaps a teacher who made you feel inferior, stupid, inept. You may continue to seek out people who can take the reins of your life because you don't believe you possibly could take those reins yourself. One thing is certain: if you think of yourself as a hopeless child, you've got a phantom presence living a very active life in your unconscious mind and giving you the message that you're a hopeless child.

6. *Do you find yourself getting depressed at a particular time every year, but you don't know why?*
"Anniversary reactions" are much more common than many people realize. Do you find yourself getting depressed, as if on cue, at Christmastime or on your birthday or at any other specific time of year, every year? If you give yourself some time—and the inner "permission" to explore your feelings about this particular anniversary reaction—you'll almost invariably discover a very specific reason for your depression. Perhaps someone abused or neglected you on a holiday; perhaps you felt particularly alone or abandoned or unfairly punished at a particular time. Perhaps someone close to you died, and, as much as you're convinced you've "gotten over it," every time the anniversary crops up you're devastated. Our anniversary reactions can be very subtle, but they indicate the presence of a phantom that, sooner or later, needs to be dealt with. Phantoms who "obviously" bother you on an anniversary often have other quieter but equally destructive ways of affecting you and your relationships throughout the rest of the year as well. An anniversary reaction

may very well be a signal that that phantom has to be acknowledged—and dealt with.

What unifies these questions—what does answering yes to them really indicate? Every question we've just discussed has to do with the fear of facing situations as they appear to be—the fear of facing life's circumstances directly. They also illustrate the "flip side" of this problem: they indicate some of the often desperate ways in which we cling to myths we think we can't survive without. Whether you idealize or vilify your parents, or can't imagine them having sex—whether you feel caught by a past affair, or can't seem to help comparing yourself or your partner to others—whether you never feel grown-up or fall victim to anniversary reactions—in each case you're responding to a *myth* or image from which you unconsciously cannot part.

However, before we can explore the root reasons for why we've chosen our particular myths, we need to see the mechanism that allows us to keep those myths so virulently alive. That mechanism is what I call a "cutoff."

▲

CUTOFFS AND WHY THEY EQUAL PHANTOM LOVER TRIANGLES

It is common for many of us to respond to rejection or to the prospect of feared change by "cutting off." What exactly does this mean?

When you are very uncomfortable with unpredictability in relationships, and especially when you resist the fact that your partner is changing, you may simply say "To hell with it!" and abruptly end the relationship. You cut that partner off, in the hope that ridding the person from your sight will banish him or her from your mind and heart. As we'll see later, however, not all cutoffs are outwardly abrupt, angry, or bitter: sometimes a painful incident from childhood makes us cut off the memory of the person who caused it. Sometimes a wonderful love experience that, for whatever reason, makes us feel uncomfortable or guilty today causes us to cut off conscious memory of the person to whom we were once attached. In all cases, cutoffs are self-protective: we attempt to rid ourselves of a person or memory that we feel is threatening.

The hard truth is, however, that cutoffs never really get rid of the "threat"—they never truly eradicate the pain we feel about being rejected or abused; they never actually ease our anger and fear about someone else's having "changed." As much as we may momentarily convince ourselves we're "free" of whomever we've cut off, all we're really doing is banishing that partner to our unconscious minds, keeping him or her, in fact, powerfully and destructively alive. Cutoffs create a terrible obstacle to our own growth; they can create powerful phantom presences—and Phantom Lover Triangles.

The fact is, cutoffs *aren't* cutoffs after all: they actually negatively *attach* us forever to people by preventing us from accepting the natural ebb and flow, the natural evolution, of our relationships with those people. The phantoms that result from these cutoffs can be very powerful, but also, as we've suggested, very insidious—hard to detect.

Confronting our phantoms is 95 percent of the task of getting rid of them. This means that becoming conscious of the ways in which we cut off to *create* our Phantom Lover Triangles is crucial. Let's look at a few real-life stories of people who've managed to do this—and begin to learn how we can increase our own consciousness.

▲

THE MAN WHO WOULDN'T GO AWAY

Celia and Jack have been married for three years, and the first time she came to see me, Celia frankly admitted that she was "bored." "I read all those articles that tell you not to expect the honeymoon to last more than two years," Celia sighed. "*Our* honeymoon didn't even last the whole honeymoon!" It wasn't that Celia didn't like Jack—she said, in fact, that she really did love him. "But it's never been a mad, passionate, head-over-heels kind of love. It's been pretty lukewarm, I guess. I don't know if the problem is me or if it's him, but somehow the security and comfort of our relationship isn't enough anymore. I need more than a pal as a husband—I want a lover, too."

Jack, Celia said, always had his priorities strongly in place— and she respected that. "I feel lucky that Jack wants to get to the top. He's being considered for partnership in one of the biggest accounting firms in New York, and he's worked damned hard to get there. I was so tired of men I had to *push* before—Jack was a relief." Who were those other men? I asked her. "Oh," Celia began vaguely, "two or three men I knew in and after college. No one all that special." She paused for a moment and frowned slightly. "Well—there *was* someone: Ron. But I don't think of him at all anymore. And thank God I don't. When I think of the *time* I spent pushing Ron to be somebody—to believe in himself. Thank God I don't have to do that with Jack. Jack is the most self-motivated man I know. Couldn't be more different from Ron." Celia paused again, and then continued in a quiet voice, "I hate thinking about those years—those wasted years. Thank God they're over."

I wondered how "over" they really were. And, in fact, when Celia later complied with my suggestion to diagram this triangle, it turned out Ron was a much bigger current force in her life than she had thought. But before she did her diagrams, I wanted her to tell me more generally what Ron had meant to her. I knew Celia needed to "exhume" this phantom to begin to realize how much force it/he still had for her.

She said she had met Ron in college, where his ambition was to be an artist—"He was perfectly content with the idea of doing odd jobs for the rest of his life so that he could devote his time to painting, making just enough money to survive." Celia said she had other plans for him. "Ron was brilliant, and I couldn't understand why he wouldn't take on more of the world—why he didn't want to achieve more. I became a sort of one-woman cheering section for him— telling him, sure, he could always do art, but why not try to make money so he could live comfortably? Somehow, I got him to come around. To the point where when I told him I was applying to graduate school in art history, he said he might try that too." He did—and eventually graduated first in his class, while Celia barely squeaked through. "It was as if I'd created some Frankenstein monster," Celia said. "He changed completely—he'd lost all interest in creating art. Now he wanted nothing more than to get ahead. Our roles reversed: instead of me pulling him, he was outdistancing me."

It turned out Ron was becoming more distant than Celia first realized. "We'd been living together since college and grad school, and I couldn't understand why, with Ron's new conserv- atism, he wasn't pushing us to get married. Whenever I brought the subject up, he got evasive." He finally told Celia why. "He said he just didn't love me the way he used to—he felt I was hold- ing him back. He'd met me when he was just an 'artist' but now he wanted more out of life. He needed to expand, meet new peo- ple. He was telling me he wasn't in love with me anymore. That's really what it was."

Celia was devastated. "I'd seen him through all the ups and downs of getting started as a museum administrator, and he was now in line to be curator of an art museum. *I* was the one who got him started in his career in the first place! It was a terrible time." Feeling hurt and rejected, she left Ron, got her own apart- ment, and got a new job—where she met Jack. "Jack was like a well-adjusted Ron, I kept telling myself. He was ambitious but he was considerate—he respected other people's feelings." Celia continued, "I just buried all memories of Ron, and until now, I haven't given him a conscious thought. And I wish I hadn't thought of him now, either!"

However, it was clear that if Celia had in fact "buried" Ron, she'd buried him alive. By attempting to cut off her feelings for him, she had "caged" him deep within herself, where he continued to exert a strong influence in her life—keeping her from feeling free to love Jack, preventing her from seeing Jack for who he really was, blocking her ability to enjoy any kind of lovemaking. The phantom she'd made of Ron was all but howling inside her.

It was time to diagram this "howling" triangle and to see why it continued to be so powerful. At first Celia couldn't accept that the following triangle was "apparent"—that it was going on *today*:

Celia

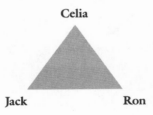

Jack   Ron

But when she wrote her feelings list and came up with the emotional and root triangles those feelings gave rise to, it sank in. Here, first, were the feelings:

I feel that:

Celia is	Jack is	Ron is
ashamed	ineffectual	arrogant
angry	distracted	selfish
lonely	insensitive	self-absorbed
hurt	in his own world	uncaring
weak	unreliable	disloyal

Her emotional triangle stacked up as follows:

Second best

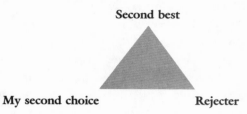

My second choice   **Rejecter**

And the root triangle of those roles brought up was clear:

Celia

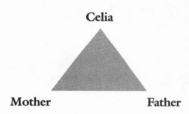

Mother   **Father**

When she expanded on her family background, there was no doubt that there were strong root-triangle reasons for Celia's present Phantom Lover Triangle. Celia's father was an absentminded mathematician who saw himself, and was treated by his wife as, a wunderkind—a brilliant professor who was above most worldly concerns and deserved the abject devotion of everyone around him. He showed little enthusiasm for or interest in Celia, who didn't share his aptitude for mathematics and wasn't the academic wonder he was. And Celia's mother clearly adored her father above anyone else (including Celia) in the family. Celia felt cut off.

In choosing Ron, she unconsciously felt she'd found a man whose raw potential she could help to nurture as her mother had helped to support her father—she'd found a man who wouldn't reject her as her father had, because *she* would be the reason for his success. Psychically, she felt she'd finally be able to get the love of her father by creating a *new* father who couldn't help but love her. Ron's rejection of her was thus unbearably painful, and the only way she knew to survive that pain was to cut Ron off. She was used to being cut off herself, and she employed the same cutting-off techniques she had experienced, as a child, from her parents.

Choosing Jack as a replacement was, so far, a feeble solution—marrying him on the rebound meant that she was still deeply attached to Ron. Jack was also, in many ways, as distant as her own father had been and as Ron had become: she was perpetuating the pattern even with him. The problem she'd come to me with—the fact that she felt no "passion" with her husband—had much deeper triangular roots than she had ever dreamed. She was haunted by at least two phantoms—the looming one of Ron, and the background ghost of her father, each telling her that she was unlovable, that she wasn't "enough."

Every relationship has a beginning, middle, and end. Unless we allow our relationships to have their seasonal evolutions—unless we *accept* those evolutions—we can't grow, whether singly or in partnership with anyone else. And when we don't grow, we atrophy: we remain stuck in an infantile relationship with the "person" we've cut off. I put "person" in quotes because when we cut someone off, we're no longer seeing that someone as a real, rounded human being; we no longer accept the inevitability of change, which means we're no longer accepting or responding to reality.

Few of us haven't harbored deep resentments against one or more people in our lives. Take a moment to think of one of your resentments—someone you're convinced hurt you, or responded to you so unfairly that, to this day, you can't "bear" to relive the episode. (Jot these thoughts down in your journal.) How do you see that person, even if the episode happened ten or twenty or more years ago? Doesn't he or she look the same as then? Don't you hear the same words, see the same face—aren't you in a kind of emotional combat with this person which is exactly like the one you last had, however long ago it was that you had it? You've just discovered a phantom intruder in your life today. You've set a highly charged episode in amber—kept it exactly as it was—and given it a potent reality it really doesn't deserve.

▲

OTHER KINDS OF CUTOFFS AND THE PHANTOMS THEY CREATE

As I suggested earlier, however, not all cutoffs are as obvious as the ones triggered by fierce resentments that we consciously acknowledge today. We can hide our phantoms from ourselves in some ingenious ways, out of self-protective urges that tell us even *thinking* about certain people is dangerous. As a result, we often find ourselves in some peculiar Phantom Lover Triangles.

Samantha, like Celia, came to me because of relationship problems with her husband. She was a woman in her mid-thirties, and she was embarrassed at first when she tried to tell me what was bothering her. "It's not that Harry isn't passionate with me," she said. "I mean, he certainly tries to be. It's just that I don't ever seem to be able to respond." Samantha had never had an orgasm with Harry, and she felt somehow guilty, as if it were her fault. Harry evidently prided himself on his lovemaking techniques, and Samantha's lack of response was deeply distressing to him.

It turned out that Samantha had had a sexually satisfying relationship early in her life—in her twenties she'd had an affair with a man, Daniel, who frequently brought her to orgasm—so she knew, she said, that she was "capable" of responding to a man more "fully." Daniel, it turned out, was married, and Samantha ended up leaving him—and "cutting him off" as completely as she could. "It was the old story. He said he was going to divorce his wife, but he kept finding excuses for putting it off. Finally I gave him an ultimatum—either her or me—and he ended up choosing her." Samantha felt hurt and ashamed for having allowed herself to become so intimate with, and dependent on, a married man. By the time she met and married Harry, she had consciously "banished" all memories of Daniel. But what she seemed also to have banished was her ability to give herself freely in sex.

When I had her do her triangle diagrams, the sources of this problem became clear. First her apparent triangle:

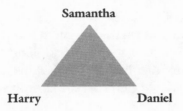

Samantha

Harry   Daniel

Then the list of feelings each triangle member brought up:

I feel that:

Samantha is	Harry is	Daniel is
"used goods"	conventional	exciting
immoral	boring	seductive
weak	stultifying	illicit
needy	unexciting	irresistible

Samantha's emotional triangle coalesced from this feelings list quickly:

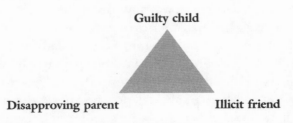

Guilty child

Disapproving parent   Illicit friend

And once she saw the feelings she had about her triangle members, her root triangle also fell into place:

Samantha

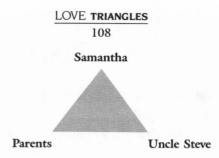

Parents   Uncle Steve

The appearance of her uncle in her root triangle was a surprise to Samantha. She was amazed to get in touch again with childhood feelings she realized she had long ago buried. She explained, "My mother had always told me that no man wants 'used goods.' I should never let a man touch me without the promise of marriage." All men, according to her mother, subscribed to a simple philosophy: "Why buy a cow when you can get the milk for free?" Samantha's father was also deeply conventional; the idea of extramarital sex was horrifying to him. "I think Daddy would never have spoken to me if he'd known about Daniel," Samantha said.

Buy why did her uncle appear as the "root" behind Daniel? "The only bright light in my life was Uncle Steve," Samantha said. "My parents disapproved of him because he was so extravagant—he used to gamble on horses, and when he had a windfall he'd come into town and shower us, and especially me, with gifts. When he left, my parents always made me give away the toys he gave me. But Uncle Steve was so full of joy and fun—I couldn't hate him the way my parents seemed to want me to." Uncle Steve had had a series of wives, all divorced, and Samantha sometimes overheard her mother and father whisper about his "affairs." "How could those women put up with him?" she remembers her mother asking. Samantha had no trouble imagining how women might fall for her uncle—and she couldn't help fantasizing herself about what it might be like to have a romance with him. When Samantha was 14 years old, Steve was sent to prison for a scam operation. She never saw him again. Thereafter feelings toward Uncle Steve were both wonderful and guilt-provoking.

When Daniel appeared in her life, both the guilt and the intoxication were reactivated. Daniel represented, as her Uncle Steve had previously, pleasure for the sake of pleasure—the idea of which was anathema to Samantha's parents. Samantha allowed herself to give way to the "intoxicating" part, but she had absorbed enough of her own parents' morality that she couldn't give way completely: she still felt there was something wrong with so much pleasure. She felt deeply that she had been irrevocably "stained" by her affair with Daniel—by the experience of letting go in such an "immoral" way.

Obviously Samantha had felt that she was "used goods" by the time she got to Harry. She'd felt ashamed of herself for "giving herself away" to a man who didn't want her for more than an affair. And yet she had enjoyed having sex with Daniel so much that she felt the need to punish herself today, by restraining herself sexually with Harry. Harry's need to bolster his own sense of himself as an adept lover by bringing Samantha to orgasm just drove Samantha more into herself: the greater his "demand" that she "enjoy" sex, the greater her unconscious resistance. It was as if, unconsciously, she was taunting herself: "How can I enjoy sex with my husband? I'm damaged goods—I don't deserve to experience sexual pleasure." Even more deeply, she was afraid to let go because the last time she'd let go she'd been rejected. She'd begun to associate sexual pleasure with danger— the danger of being abandoned.

As Celia discovered, while the phantom in Samantha's apparent triangle was clearly the ex-lover she had tried to cut off (Daniel), more deeply Samantha was responding to messages her mother and father had instilled: that sex was dangerous—it made you vulnerable, it "damaged" you so that no man would offer to take care of you. Just as strongly, she got the message that she wasn't entitled to pleasure for its own sake.

To free herself from the influence of her apparent Phantom Lover Triangle, she needed to acknowledge that she was still heeding these messages, which means she needed to face the root triangle with her parents that kept her phantom so firmly in place. Again, we'll come to the process that helped Samantha (and Celia) do this kind of "exorcism" in a moment, but first let's consider some of the general issues that Phantom Lover Triangles force all of us to confront.

▲

LEARNING TO LIVE IN THE PRESENT

Accepting that the past is the past and that we have the resources we need, right now, to make free and satisfying choices in the present may sound like pap—we have all heard we must live in the present and "let go" of the past. However, it's one of the most difficult and necessary tasks any of us faces. The phantom created by the cutoff person in your life can direct you in the subtlest, least detectable ways, especially when, as is almost always the case, that phantom has links to phantoms in your *root* triangle. It's pretty much invariable that if you react to relationships today by cutting off when you can't tolerate the idea of anyone changing, you learned that cutoff technique in childhood.

Celia knew what it was to feel cut off because it's how she always felt as a little girl—she was locked into a pattern whose influence she had no idea was so strong. Samantha cut off Daniel instinctively, because the message she'd internalized from her own parents was that *she'd* be cut off if she ever "gave herself away" before marriage. Other people may have different motives for cutting off. One client of mine, Jeannette, had a very clear Phantom Lover Triangle connecting her lover, Al, with her repressed memory of a male baby-sitter who had fondled her sexually when she was a little girl. She could never respond freely in sex because unconsciously she mixed Al up with that baby-sitter whenever they had sex. Jeannette had done everything she consciously could to block out memories of this baby-sitter—to cut him off—but the experience with him had so traumatized her that he was inextricably (if unconsciously) bound up in every sexual thought or experience she had. This is an example of a Phantom Lover Triangle that is also the root triangle: Jeannette's baby-sitter was the root cause of her anxiety about sex, as well as a very powerful "presence" in her life with Al today.

How have Jeannette, Samantha, and Celia managed not only to come to terms with their Phantom Lover Triangles but to have freer, more satisfying love relationships? And how can you learn to do the same thing? By facing fears—and their phantoms—in some productive new ways. As you'll discover in the next two sections, identifying the phantom in a Phantom Lover Triangle can also give you the key to exorcising it.

▲

DIAGNOSIS: IDENTIFYING YOUR PHANTOM TRIANGLE

Identifying the phantom presence that makes up the third point of your Phantom Lover Triangle means asking yourself some questions we haven't yet considered.

First of all, you need to investigate who in your life you've cut off. This often isn't as easy as simply going back over your life and considering each significant person in it. When we decide to hide a phantom we usually do a very good job, and discovering who that phantom is usually isn't achieved by the frontal assault of direct self-questioning. We usually have to turn to our feelings to begin to find (and then exorcise) the ghost. The best way I know of doing this is recovering what I call the "key scene."

Finding the Key Scene

Phantoms usually can be found in certain "key scenes"— memories of events that happened early in your life and that you may have buried, but that still have a great deal of unconscious impact on your life today. You can discover your key scenes by paying close attention to your feelings. First, open up your journal. Then, pen in hand, ask yourself:

▲ When I feel angry, depressed, fearful, or resentful, does anything come to mind? Who or what do I flash on in the heat of one of these painful emotions?

If a specific person immediately comes to mind, more strongly than any other person, you may have your phantom right away. But it's perhaps more likely that you won't "see" any human being at all when you first allow yourself to free-associate in this way. You may instead remember an event or a scene. If you do, hold on to it, and ask yourself:

▲ What about this scene is causing me to feel the way I do?

▲ Who has made me feel shame or sadness or fear or anger? What did he/she/they do? What did I do?

Allow yourself to absorb the impact of this scene—replay it as vividly as you can. Eventually, if you stay with your feelings and the scene that your feelings call up for you, the cast of characters and the nature of the event will be clear. Soon you should be able to "see" your phantom clearly. Be prepared to feel resistance: you haven't hidden this phantom from yourself for nothing. In fact, generally you've identified someone you've cut off when your response to the memory of that person is something like Celia's was when I first asked her about Ron ("I hate thinking about it"). Whenever you say something like "I'd rather not talk about it," you've almost invariably happened on a topic that urgently *needs* to be talked about. It's very likely that the memory you least want to face is the one you most need to face, because it holds your phantom.

Once you've found your phantom, you can complete our triangle diagram process:

1. Draw your apparent triangle, including you, the phantom you've just found, and the primary partner with whom you

haven't been able to achieve full intimacy because of the phantom.

2. List your feelings, as we've done before:

I feel that:

I am	**My partner is**	**Phantom is**

3. Consider the list of possible feeling themes we set out in chapter 4 (page 59) to see, on the basis of the feelings you've just listed, which theme applies most strongly to each of the triangle's members. (As always, feel free to come up with any feeling themes that occur to you but that we have not already listed.) Now draw your emotional triangle.

4. Reflect on who these themes remind you of most strongly from your past to come up with your root triangle. The phantom you've found in your apparent triangle may also be in your root triangle—or the phantom may have another deeper source (as Samantha discovered when her Uncle Steve came to mind as the "root" behind Daniel, her ex-lover). Let your feelings and the spontaneous memories they elicit be your guide.

Now that you've discovered your phantom and the connections between past and present these diagrams have shown you, you're ready to take a look at what you can do to exorcise that phantom in your relationship today.

▲

TREATMENT: MOVING FROM YOUR KEY SCENE TO LIFE WITH YOUR PARTNER TODAY

You've learned something important by allowing yourself to follow your feelings to the key scene you identified above: you've discovered "trigger" emotions that make you vulnerable to your phantom's presence. Anger, resentment, fear, depression, and anxiety are common trigger feelings in Phantom Lover Triangles—but as painful as they are, you can always use them to get back to the key scene you identified above (or any other new key scenes that may come up for you—it's likely you've got several tied to your phantom). Why would you want to go back to that key scene—especially if it causes you so much pain?

It's only by allowing yourself to feel your fears and face your pain that you have a chance of getting over them. It's only by looking the phantom in the face that you can drain it of its power. Try the following when your phantom trigger feelings start to overwhelm you again:

1. Allow yourself to return to your key scene. Visualize it in complete detail: allow yourself to see the players in it, hear what they say, feel the feelings, relive its reality, write it down in your journal in full detail.

2. Reaffirm that your key scene no longer has power over you today. Recognize the difference between your past as you see it in your key scene and your present, today; realize that as an adult, you now have more resources and skills to deal with life than you did as a child. Affirm to yourself again and again: *No one in my past has power over me today.* Leave the image in your journal—walk away free of its burden.

3. Bring your "live" partner into the picture. Having faced your phantom and your old fears, having affirmed that they no longer need direct you today, remind yourself that you have options with your primary partner today that have nothing to do with your past. You can forge an entirely new relationship *between the two of you.*

This three-step Phantom Lover Triangle process can be amazingly effective. Whenever the old anxiety crops up, put yourself through the key scene it calls up vividly enough to bid it farewell—to remind you that it need have no power over you today. Then reflect on your current relationship, affirming the choices you have to face each other as the person each of you is now. With enough practice, you'll discover that your phantom no longer takes the same space as he or she used to take in your relationship—or your life.

7

THE ROTATING DATE TRIANGLE

As you might expect from its name, the Rotating Date Triangle can keep you spinning. It does what we have learned all other triangles do—it gives you ways to escape one-to-one intimacy—but it does more: it keeps you from even a *semblance* of commitment to one person. What are its three points?

1. You.
2. One of a series of virtually interchangeable love partners.
3. A third "restraining force," sometimes a competing love partner, or your child or a parent (actual or internalized), who you consciously or unconsciously feel keeps you from making a full commitment to any *one* person in your life.

The typical Rotating Date Triangulator doesn't have to be a Casanova—ranging from conquest to conquest, forever fleeing any suggestion of permanency. It might be a single mother who dates man after man but who feels that no man could possibly be right as the father of her children. It might be someone who appears to be actively seeking a "committed" mate but always seems to end up with prospects to whom the very idea of commitment is anathema. Rotating Date Triangulators may be the most vocal proponents of commitment—"All I really want is to settle down with the right person!" they often cry—but "something" always seems to keep them from meeting that "right" person. No one ever seems to measure up.

Like every triangle we've seen and will see in this book, however, Rotating Date Triangles can be subtle, and we typically have a lot of denial that we're in them. Take the following quiz, and see if this triangle applies to you. Put your answers in your journal.

▲
THE ROTATING DATE TRIANGLE QUIZ

1. Do you often have a hard time making decisions, even about simple things like what clothing to wear or what food to choose on a restaurant menu?

2. Do you maintain a wide network of friends with whom you find yourself "flirting" to keep open the possibility of romantic involvement?

3. Do you experience "wanderlust"—wanting to change a job as soon as you've gotten it, convincing yourself that things would be better somewhere else?

4. Do you feel that most of the people you know are childish—and/or can't be trusted?

5. Was there a member of your family when you were growing up who always made life difficult for you—who regularly brought tension and fear into your home environment?

6. Is it essential to you to be up on the latest book, restaurant, film, play, vacation spot, entertainer, or "guru"?

Let's take a brief look at why answering yes to any of these questions indicates a tendency to "rotate."

1. Do you often have a hard time making decisions, even about simple things like what clothing to wear or what food to choose on a restaurant menu?
Occasional indecisiveness is perfectly normal, but when you feel hobbled by the prospect of choosing *anything* no matter how trivial the choice, it's virtually certain that you'll have a hard time making a commitment to a love partner. You may instead find yourself allowing other people to make decisions for you—even in love.

A woman who is indecisive about everything in her life may simply say yes to the first man who asks her to marry him, finding out too late that she's "chosen" the wrong man, or rather allowed the wrong man to choose *her*. Many Rotating Date Triangulators emerge from this kind of bad relationship only to get into another, entered into with equally poor judgment.

2. Do you maintain a wide network of friends with whom you find yourself "flirting" to keep open the possibility of romantic involvement?
Making sure you've got "options" often means making sure you've got "exits." When you can't bear the thought of cutting anyone off as a romantic possibility—when you need to see everyone you meet as a potential love partner—it's virtually certain that you employ the rotating-date mode of triangulating. There's nothing wrong with occasional flirting—it can be fun, and tantalizing, and can get a relationship going in some delightful ways—but when flirting is reflexive, you're generally holding something *back* reflexively. Flirting may appear to promise intimacy, but in fact it can enable you to withhold it. The flirtatious gesture is actually sometimes much more distancing than inviting.

3. **Do you experience "wanderlust"—wanting to change a job as soon as you've gotten it, convincing yourself that things would be better somewhere else?**

If you tend to feel that the grass is always greener somewhere else, it's highly probable that you're no stranger to the Rotating Date Triangle. As one Rotating Date Triangulator put it, "When I'm out dancing with a woman, I can't keep from wanting to dance with every other woman in the place—at the same time!" No job, home, geographical place, or climate is ever quite adequate to Rotating Date Triangulators—never mind the people in their lives. This doesn't mean that all such triangulators dart around actually making radical change after radical change (although some do). Sometimes the ache for something different takes place in the imagination, à la Walter Mitty. But even armchair "rotators" make themselves miserable—even if they "decide" (i.e., resign themselves) to stay where they are, or with the partners they have.

4. **Do you feel that most of the people you know are childish—and/or can't be trusted?**

We dealt with the theme of this question earlier, in chapter 2, when we discussed one of the first "Triangulator Predictor Quiz" questions I asked you ("Do you think 'all men' or 'all women' are backstabbers—do you believe you can't trust them?"). But it's an issue that particularly pertains to the Rotating Date Triangulator.

The point we made before applies here. If you think most or all of the people you know are untrustworthy or are crucially lacking in other areas, you set yourself up for a continual need to *replace* those people in your life. And when you're convinced that most or all the people you know are "childish," what you're really saying is that you don't know anyone who is capable and strong enough to take care of you. These kinds of blanket judgments about "all" the people you know are, in reality, a kind of self-protection—protecting yourself from ever risking too much intimacy with any one person. But because (like the rest of the human beings on this planet) you have a *need* for intimacy, they are also judgments that compel you to seek "someone better"—again and again. If you're a Rotating Date Triangulator, you find yourself in a particularly vicious circle: doomed to seek what you've already unconsciously decided you can never find.

5. *Was there a member of your family when you were growing up who always made life difficult for you—who regularly brought tension and fear into your home environment?*

When you grow up in an attitude of tension and fear, it's natural not to feel you can trust the people around you who you perceive are causing that tension and fear. Children of alcoholics are frequently Rotating Date Triangulators, as is anyone who suffered any form of abuse or mistreatment or chronic insecurity as a child. This abuse may not always or perhaps ever have been physical. Sometimes a "significant family member"—usually a parent—can communicate tension and induce fear simply because the messages he or she sends out about behavior expected of you aren't clear. And when you're not clear about what the "rules" are in your family, it means you're not clear how to get the love and attention you need. As a result, when you grow up you can't help but feel a terrible and terrifying insecurity about where your next "love" is coming from.

All of this quite naturally sets you up to be wary with any subsequent love partner: something in you doesn't dare trust that your partner will really give you what you want, even when your partner says he or she will. And so you go from partner to partner, hoping the next one will give you the cure-all feeling of safety and security and being loved that you were after as a child.

6. **Is** *it essential to you to be up on the latest book, restaurant, film, play, vacation spot, entertainer, or "guru"?*
We've already discovered that a crucial motivation in most triangulators is to look *outside* themselves for something to fill what is really a void *inside* themselves. People who immerse themselves in what's "in" or "hot" or "now" are poignant examples of this desperate urge. They urgently seek from the outside world enough meaning, distraction, entertainment, and validation (if they know what's "happening," won't they be more attractive to others?) to fill that inner void. They value "things" or "places" as a defense against feeling the anxiety of an intimate relationship. In a sense the motivation here is similar to the one we explored in our previous question: you can never "trust" that what you have now—or the person in your life now—could ever be enough. There must be something better, you keep telling yourself, and if you can only hold out long enough, you'll find it. Unfortunately, what you often find when you continue to "hold out" in this way is that your life has passed without you ever having experienced one moment of real intimacy.

▲

KEEPING OPTIONS FROM TURNING INTO EXITS

What all of these questions—and the main issue faced by the Rotating Date Triangulator—have to do with is the problem of turning options into exits. Going from love partner to love partner may give you a transitory feeling of "freedom"—you may tell yourself that you're simply exercising "options" in your life because you want to. However, when you "exit" situations and relationships because you can't *help* but feel that the next opportunity "has" to be better, you ultimately end up exiting any real chance of lasting intimacy with anyone. What you've been calling options are actually escape hatches—relationships you only get into with the assurance that you can get out of them.

How do you stop the fearful urge to "rotate" from partner to partner, setting up one triangle after another?

You need to face two main destructive assumptions that, if you're a Rotating Date Triangulator, I guarantee you have about yourself and your relationships:

1. Love is a burden—a responsibility I couldn't possibly meet.

2. I can't trust anyone to provide me with what I need.

These assumptions not only provide the deepest reasons Rotating Date Triangulators triangulate; they also indicate the "rotator's" deepest fears. Seeing love as a burden also usually dovetails with the rotator's general lack of trust: how could you "trust" anyone you "love" to give you what you need if you see love as an onerous responsibility?

Let's look at some real-life examples of how you can face—and triumph over—these two assumptions, assumptions that may be locking you into this triangle's endless permutations. I promise that once you start to do this, you will begin to lose the urge to rotate and start to find the intimacy you're always been convinced you never *could* find with one other person.

▲
LIGHTENING THE BURDEN OF LOVE

Len is a well-known public personality, and his charm is almost legendary. He has enormous appeal to women and has had a number of well-publicized relationships with some of today's most beautiful and accomplished women. He was, in fact, such an apparent success with women and in his career that I was more than a little puzzled when he came to see me. What could be bothering him?

At first, it seemed to be some version of a "midlife crisis." Len was forty-two, and apart from what he described as a brief and ill-advised marriage in his twenties to a woman he'd met in college, he hadn't been able to settle down with any woman. "I still feel like a kid," Len told me. "Some part of me doesn't understand why I can't just continue to fool around as I did in my twenties and thirties—just go from woman to woman. What's wrong with that?" He seemed almost to want me to tell him that something was wrong with it—obviously because he'd told himself over and over what he himself felt was wrong. So I asked him what *he* felt was wrong with fooling around.

"I guess I'm starting to realize I'm *not* a kid anymore. And I'm starting to feel lonely in a strange way. It's not that I couldn't be with a different woman every night—but I'm starting to want to be with the *same* woman every night. And I can't for the life of me imagine who that could be." Len also told me that for the first time he could remember, women were turning him down— because of his reputation as someone who couldn't make a commitment. "It's a little embarrassing. I imagine that women don't look at me the way they used to—a young guy they can have a good time with. Now they're starting to see me as someone sort of pathetic, a guy who pretends he's a kid but should really act his age." Acting his "age" clearly meant, to Len, "settling down"—getting married. "But I'm terrified. I've never allowed myself to really think what life would be like with just one woman. As much as part of me wants that to happen, another part of me is terrified."

The typical pattern for Len seemed to be that he'd become infatuated with one woman, think about her all the time, shower her with attention, and then notice some tiny flaw—"Sometimes it's a pet phrase a woman may use that gets on my nerves, sometimes it's something physical, like a tiny gap in her teeth, or the shape of her chin or her nose"—and the flaw would start to assume outrageous proportions. "After a while, all I'm able to notice about the woman is what I don't like about her. And so my eye roves till someone new pops up. Which never takes long." Len frequently found himself simultaneously at the end of one relationship and at the beginning of another. "It would be like sunset on the left and sunrise on the right. There was always a new day—a new horizon—a new woman. I really don't know how to live any other way."

But because this mode wasn't working out as well as it had in the past—both because he felt a need for a deeper kind of intimacy than he had ever allowed himself and because women who knew his track record of brief liaisons were starting to turn him down—Len had come to me for help. "Why can't I get married like other guys," he asked me, "and be happy about it?"

To find the answer to this question, Len would have to get down to some roots that, at the moment, he had no idea were there.

I had Len do our triangle exercise, drawing his current apparent triangle, starting by labeling the three points with his own name and the names of the two women with whom he was involved at the moment (Angela was the woman on the way out and Carol his new infatuation):

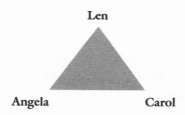

Then I had him think of and list the feelings Angela and Carol each brought up for him.

He wrote the following:

I feel that:

Len is	Angela is	Carol is
misunderstood	too serious	fun-loving
pressured	disapproving	adventurous
wants to enjoy life	workaholic	lives for now

Len had some interesting insights when he gave himself a moment to really look at these lists. More than interesting—they nearly blew him away. First, he said, "I never realized I saw myself as such a victim—'pressured, misunderstood.' I mean, on the face of it, I've always gotten pretty much what I wanted!" When he looked at what he'd written under Angela's and Carol's names, he was equally astonished. "Do you know," he said, "I used to think of Angela, when I first met her, as all the things I'm calling Carol? I never realized that before!" Len said that what he now found "serious" and "disapproving" and "workaholic" in Angela he had once seen as "passion for her work, excited and adventurous in her life, ready and willing to take risks." What had happened?

Even from this simple exercise Len began to see that maybe it wasn't that Angela—or all the women before Angela—had changed so much. Maybe it was his own *perception* that had changed. But what was changing it? Why did he seem to feel compelled to transform every woman he started out loving into someone he couldn't abide?

I asked Len to take the next step: to erase "Carol" and "Angela" and "Len" from the points of the triangle he had just drawn and, after looking at the lists of feelings he'd written, replace those names with summary feeling themes from the list on page 59, or any themes that occurred to him which weren't on the list. This took some thought, but eventually Len wrote the following:

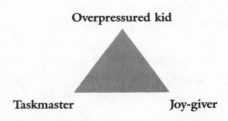

Overpressured kid

Taskmaster   Joy-giver

The dynamics of his apparent triangle were suddenly crystal-clear to Len—and to me. He felt torn between an oppressive "taskmaster" and a savior-like "joy-giver." The fact that at forty-two years old he experienced all this as an "overpressured kid" clearly pointed to the deep roots these roles had for him. Now he needed to take a good, hard look at these roots. Who did his feeling themes remind him of—who, most strongly and distantly in his past, did they call up for him?

Len didn't need to think long to come up with the names. He quickly drew the following root triangle:

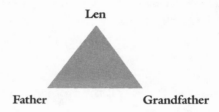

Len

Father   **Grandfather**

He now told me the story attached to these names. Len was born and spent his boyhood in rural Montana. His father spent long, hard hours farming, and Len had almost nothing to do with him, growing up, that didn't involve endless chores. But his grandfather, who was retired, was a source of endless fun: he taught Len funny songs, how to do country dances, how to hunt and whittle and enjoy life. It was clear that the only way Len had learned to relate to his own father was by fulfilling his many arduous duties on the farm, and the main way he related to his grandfather was to have fun with him. It wasn't a secret which man he preferred spending his time with.

But, Len told me, there was another root triangle that wasn't as "old" as this—but that the feeling themes he'd come up with reminded him of just as strongly. So I asked him to list the points of that triangle. For the "Taskmaster" role he wrote, "My brother," and for "Joy-giver" he wrote, "My sister." "My brother," Len said, "does this 'helpless act' really well—he always has. He's always in some sort of money trouble, always getting sick, always getting involved in lousy jobs and with terrible women—and I'm always called on to bail him out." Len's sister had a very different effect. "Janie is a little irresponsible, too," Len said, "but that doesn't matter. She doesn't come running to me for help all the time—she gets herself out of her own scrapes. I love her—I have a great time visiting her and talking to her. She enjoys life just as Granddad did, and I always feel at ease with her."

Len discovered that he had two very strong root triangles that had given him a horror of "responsibility"—which, because he associated it with his father and brother, he thought of as an onerous burden—and a compelling desire for "fun," which his grandfather and sister symbolized and he quite naturally found far more preferable.

But more deeply, Len realized that he associated *love* with that burdensome sense of "responsibility." His mother had died when he was a little boy, and unconsciously he blamed her for leaving him. He associated his father's grimness with the loss of his mother as well. "If that was what long-term marital 'love' got you—all that hard work and loss and bleakness—what good was it?" This doomed sense of love was simply corroborated by his brother's experience with women—"He was always so miserable whether he was involved with a woman or not"—and by his own brief "ill-advised" marriage.

In short, he deeply felt that "love" was a terrible burden to be avoided at all costs. The only thing you could count on—and then only fleetingly—was "fun."

Identifying his root and apparent triangles was enormously illuminating to Len. He began to sense it was his own assumptions that have held him back, and that those assumptions didn't come from nowhere. He can have compassion for his urge to flee at the first signs of a woman's desire for commitment. He's begun to see that his extreme intolerance for certain "flaws" in the women he goes out with are in fact excuses he gives himself not to get deeply involved. And he now practices "crossing the street" when the reflexive urge to "cut off" a woman rears its head—making sure he takes some time out to see if what he's really reacting to is his own fear of getting involved. If he realizes that he *is* reacting to that fear, he's begun to do something the old Perfect Lover Len wouldn't have dreamed of doing. He actually *talks* about his fears, right then and there, with the woman he's afraid of.

This takes enormous trust—which brings us to the next step in the process of getting over the Rotating Date Triangle syndrome. To truly allow himself to let go and give himself more freely to a love partner, Len has had to learn how to deal with the second assumption I identified earlier on: the damaging idea that you can't trust anyone to give you what you want. Let's take a look at another story to see how one woman learned to face this assumption and overcome it. Len is learning to do what she did—and you can, too.

▲
LEARNING TO TRUST

Helen, now in her early thirties, was married for seven years in her twenties. She and her husband, Bill, had a child, Bill Jr., whom she raised pretty much on her own. "Bill always paid alimony and child support," she told me when she came to see me, "but that was about it. He was too busy raising another family with Lois, the woman he married right after we broke up. I don't feel bad about it, though. I really didn't want his interference bringing Billy up." Helen told me that almost from the first day they were married, they fought. "It seemed that everything either of us did got on the other's nerves." The marriage was, both of them decided, a mistake—and they parted, if not "amicably," then at least with the full acceptance that they needed to part.

In the past several years Helen has dated dozens of men, but because she'd dedicated her life to raising her son, she never took any of these dates "seriously." Some of these men were people friends of hers had introduced her to. "Most of my friends are married, and it seems there's nothing that makes a married person more uncomfortable than a single woman—especially a single mother." Sometimes she'd meet a man at work or through the single parents' group she occasionally attended. But Helen kept herself firmly in check. "I didn't have time for all that romantic nonsense while bringing up Billy. And I couldn't believe—not really—that any man would want to get involved with a single mother. So I just blocked that part of me off."

Helen had come to me now because she realized that she wanted to open up the part of herself she'd "blocked off." She was lonely for companionship—she found herself wanting intimacy she realized she'd never really had with a man, not even when she was married. "But I still feel blocked," she said. "I freeze up when a man shows more than mild interest in me. When I finally do allow myself to date, I almost always find myself dating two men at once, just to keep things from getting too intense. If a man I go out with knows I'm seeing someone else, it seems to keep things casual. Why am I so afraid of getting more intimate?"

Helen's apparent Rotating Date Triangle was quite clear: its points were made up of Helen, Billy, and the series of men she dated but never allowed herself to get serious with:

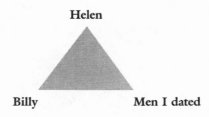

When I asked her to write down the feelings each "point" brought up for her, she came up with the following:

I feel that:

Helen is	Billy is	Men I dated are
wary	trusting	unpredictable
conservative	needy	difficult
lonely	center of my life	not to be trusted

Now, as in previous exercises we've seen, I asked Helen to erase the names on her triangle and replace them with the emotional themes she felt each expressed. It was hard for her to condense her feelings into single-word descriptions—doing this for herself was especially hard. "I've never thought of myself as emotionally consistent," Helen said. But when she looked at the list of possibilities (the suggested feeling-theme list I offered on page 59), it became clear. In fact, once she decided on her own theme ("Caretaker"), the other two themes fell easily into place. She was now able to come up with the following:

Caretaker

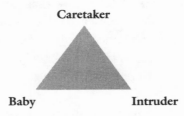

Baby   **Intruder**

Who in Helen's past life did these feeling themes call up most clearly? A little free association served Helen well. She was able after only a few moments' thought to draw her root triangle:

Mother

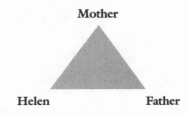

Helen   **Father**

When a triangulator makes this kind of connection, astonishment is generally the result—and Helen was no exception. "Why, it's as if I've re-created my childhood all over again!"

Helen told me a little about that childhood. Her father, Al, was a powerful personality—witty, talented, and attractive—but, Helen said, "terribly irresponsible. He made a fair amount of money as a salesman but he spent it foolishly and now he's got almost nothing—even though he's in his late sixties, he can't retire because he can't afford to." Helen's mother made no secret of her criticism of Al—though Helen also knew her mother was greatly attracted to him. "You couldn't ignore my father, and his get-rich-quick schemes were always so glamorous and plausible that for years the family kept falling for them. But while some of them worked, most of them didn't—and, well, you just couldn't trust my father about anything."

Helen told me that she never knew for sure, but she always had the feeling her father had cheated on her mother. He was always going away on business trips that seemed unnecessary. Her mother never said anything about it, but Helen noticed that whenever the subject of infidelity came up on the TV or radio or in a magazine, her mother would look uncomfortable and turn either the channel or the page. "I grew up feeling that my father was very powerful but somehow also very dangerous. I could never tell what he felt about me. He'd blow hot and cold, hugging me and bringing me home wonderful gifts one day, ignoring me or yelling at me the next." The bottom line for Helen was, again, simply this: "You couldn't trust him."

It was now astonishingly clear to Helen that she had learned to play her mother's "wary, lonely" role and that she lavished so much protective care on Billy in the psychic attempt to make baby Helen feel safe and loved and protected. Finding the "men I dated" unpredictable, dangerous, and "not to be trusted" was no longer surprising either: clearly she saw all men as her father. "I've trapped myself for all these years in this web!" she exclaimed. "Do I have the strength to get out of it?"

Learning to open yourself to trust takes patience—and practice. Now that Helen recognizes the pattern she was clinging to in her life and has begun to appreciate some of the reasons for it, she has enough awareness to begin to check her reflexive responses when they automatically flare up. As Len learned, and as the other triangulators we've met in this book have learned, you can always "cross the street" and detach for a moment, to give yourself the time and space to *decide* how you want to respond. For Helen, this translates into "sitting with the fear" until it passes—which (to her amazement) it always does.

▲
DIAGNOSIS: DETERMINING YOUR ROTATING DATE TRIANGLE

Determining the third point or the second and third points of a Rotating Date Triangle means, first, understanding that the "rotator" generally perceives relationships in one of two ways. You may rotate with two fixed points and one "general" one, as Helen did (the three points of her apparent triangle were Helen, her son, Billy, and "men I date"), or with only one "fixed point"—you—and two ever-changing second and third points (as in Len's case: Angela and Carol were simply the women he happened to be involved with at the moment).

To establish if yours is a "two-corner" or a "one-corner" Rotating Date Triangle, ask yourself the following questions (and remember to write the answers in your journal):

▲ Am I involved with two people at once right now, and do I find that I tend to be involved with more than one person at a time?

▲ If I'm involved with only one partner right now, do I think of that partner as simply one more in a string of partners, all of whom seem alike?

If you answered yes to the first question, you've got a two-corner Apparent Triangle; if you answered yes to the second question, you're still a rotator, but you'll need to fill in a third presence, too. This presence may be, as it was for Helen, your child, or it might be a friend or a family member.

Whichever it is, you're now ready to complete your diagram process. Open up your journal and:

1. Draw your apparent triangle, including you and your two rotating dates, or you and the current rotating date and the third presence that appears to you to be involved.

2. List your feelings, in the "I feel that" way we've been using:

I feel that:

I am   **Rotating date is**   **Third presence is**

3. Consider our feeling-theme list on page 59 and see which feeling applies to each presence in the triangle (as always, come up with new themes if the ones on our list don't apply). Now draw your emotional triangle.

4. Reflect on who these feeling themes remind you of most strongly from your past to come up with your root triangle.

▲

TREATMENT: TAKING RESPONSIBILITY

Fearing the "responsibility" of love and believing that "you can't trust anyone" are the greatest obstacles plaguing Rotating Date Triangulators, but each obstacle can be diminished—and your need to "rotate" can diminish, too. How?

First, you need to face what you're afraid of when you feel the impulse to run from responsibility in a relationship. You need to answer, as honestly as you can, the following questions:

▲ What do I fear most in this relationship?

▲ What responsibility do I believe I cannot meet?

Let's say you answer that you can't imagine being "committed" to one person over a long period of time, that the responsibility of caring for another person in a long-term relationship terrifies you. Once you've isolated this fear (or any other fear you've been able to isolate), follow this exercise:

1. Take a look at your root triangle again.
2. Ask yourself if you felt the same fear you're feeling now in your relationship with the presences in your root triangle.
3. Make a list of the differences between the situation in your root triangle and your situation today. For example:

Then	Now
I was helpless.	I'm an adult.
My father was abusive.	I don't have to stand for abuse.
My mother neglected me.	I can choose people who won't neglect me today.

4. In light of your "Now" list, affirm your ability to meet the responsibility you were so afraid of in your relationship today.

This four-step process is a way of proving to yourself that you *can* bear the responsibility of love, that you can learn to trust someone else in love. It will allow you to engage in your relationship—affirming that you have the resources to meet each moment of your relationship and your life without bolting in fear.

Not that the urge to bolt won't rear up again, but when it does, there are ways to check yourself, keep yourself from rotating by reflex. For example, when you're uncomfortable in your current relationship and you can feel yourself scouting around for—and finding—another attractive partner across the room, you can stop and remind yourself that whoever this person is, he or she is not a magic cure-all but has all the flaws of every other human being, and what you *don't* need now are the complications of another imperfect relationship! Remind yourself of the good feelings you've had with your present partner, even though you may not be feeling them at the moment.

Perhaps an even greater help might be repeating the following "mantra" when you become conscious of the *fear* that all Rotating Date Triangulators feel underneath the impulse to bolt. Remind yourself what you learned in your triangle diagram about your root triangle, and repeat the following affirmations to yourself:

> I am strong.
> I cannot be hurt.
> I cannot be overpowered.

The result of all this is that you'll eventually discover that you don't need to run away anymore. You won't need to rotate from partner to partner out of fear. You'll be able to choose to stay right where you are—with yourself, and with whatever partner you're learning to trust and love.

However, when you free yourself of the opportunity to exit, you may experience a sadness, almost like a mourning period—you might feel as though you lost something. But eventually the true freedom of intimacy will overcome the empty freedom that comes from turning options into exits.

8

THE MEMBERS OF THE FAMILY TRIANGLE

IN A SENSE, EVERY TRIANGLE WE'VE SO FAR EXPLORED HAS INVOLVED "MEM-BERS OF THE FAMILY"—CERTAINLY members of the family almost always crop up in our root triangles. Again, if the first, most important relationship you knew involved you, your mother, and your father, it's no longer any wonder that that initial triad has had so much force and directs you (if largely unconsciously) even today.

But sometimes members of the family wreak havoc not only because of our subconscious reactions to them, set in early childhood—they can be all too much a part of our lives in damaging ways right now. In fact, this kind of triangle can have a double hold on you: it's common for the family member who appears in your apparent triangle to have been in your root triangle, too! And it's not always a mother or father who continues to exert undue influence in your love relationships, either: siblings, cousins, or grandparents can affect us in some extraordinarily powerful ways too—ways of which, more than likely, you're completely unaware.

You can be in a Members of the Family Triangle if you continually find yourself comparing your partner to your brother or sister or a parent—but you may also be in this kind of triangle if you assiduously *avoid* any mention of or comparisons to your family. See if this triangle traps you by answering the following questions. If you answer yes even once, you've got a family tie that bears looking at. Put the answers in your journal before you turn this page.

▲

THE MEMBERS OF THE FAMILY TRIANGLE QUIZ

1. Do you feel guilty when good things happen to you?
2. Do you rarely or never speak to certain family members, whether or not you're "angry" with them?
3. Do you tend to play down your successes in your family?
4. Do you feel it's hard to get people to listen to you?
5. Do you rely on a parent or other family member to fill you in on news about the rest of the family?
6. Do you usually wait until your back is against the wall before you make a decision?

As you've seen before, questions indicating a tendency to triangulate are always a little slippery—and this is never more so than in the Members of the Family Triangle. Let's take a look at why I've asked these questions and why answering yes to them means you've got a family presence intruding on your primary love relationship even if you're not aware you do.

1. *Do you feel guilty when good things happen to you?*
This kind of irrational guilt often proceeds from a variety of feelings you may have had early on: that one parent liked you better

than he or she liked the other parent; that you shouldn't "out-shine" any family member (aspire to be more or earn more than your parents, for example); or some variant of sibling rivalry—feeling guilt at experiencing good fortune today may betray the guilt you felt when you got something a sibling didn't back in your childhood. Even if you're an only child, you may still be reacting "guiltily" at the memory of having gotten something that one or another parent didn't (only children react to parents as parents *and* siblings). Other family members may or may not have encouraged you to feel guilty about getting "the best piece"—but the net effect is that you feel you got away with something you "shouldn't" have. When this guilt is strong enough to persist into adulthood, it's a clear indication that you're still responding to a strong family presence—one sure to intrude in any one-to-one relationship you get into today.

2. Do you rarely or never speak to certain family members, whether or not you're "angry" with them?
This question is a bit more obvious, especially in light of what we've learned about "cutting off." Whenever you attempt to cut off a family member by not speaking to him or her, you are in effect very closely bound to that person, even if it is a tie more subconscious than conscious. Our resentments toward certain relatives can create strong and often destructive effects in our love relationships. At times, we displace that resentment inappropriately, often toward someone close who has nothing to do with the real source. Even if you are not conscious of negative feelings, if you still find yourself almost never communicating with a family member, it is highly probable that you have unfinished business with him or her that needs to be explored (although not necessarily directly). The issue, moreover, could be blocking your path to intimacy and other relationships in your life.

3. Do *you tend to play down your successes in your family?*
If you're afraid to tell family members about your successes, it frequently means that deep inside you're afraid of their rage— afraid they'll somehow retaliate out of jealousy, somehow "get" you for surpassing them. It may be that you learned to be frightened of drawing attention to yourself as a child—and you've now internalized that fear to make you reticent about sharing success with your family today. (This is a very common reaction, particularly when so many of us are baby-boom children, growing up with what our parents "never had.") It makes many people extremely uncomfortable to "flaunt" their success in front of their siblings, too—for similar reasons to those we explored in the first question: we feel "guilty" about having something they don't, and frightened of what we project will be their rage. All of it boils down to having a strong family presence in the middle of your life today—and not a healing presence.

4. Do *you feel it's hard to get people to listen to you?*
If you feel it's an effort to capture anyone's attention, you're undoubtedly responding to a family background in which it really *was* hard to get listened to. The problem is, you're continuing to respond to old, inappropriate expectations when you assume you won't be heard by anyone you meet *today.* You may also—in fact you probably do—choose people who *don't* listen very well, people you've chosen in the unconscious attempt to corroborate your childhood view of yourself as unworthy. Since most of us are experts at zeroing in on people who will corroborate our own self-views, if our self-views are negative, it's no wonder that we end up with people who behave negatively in our lives. The force urging us to make these choices is, however, always a "member of the family," and any relationship we get into is guaranteed to turn into a triangle, with that "member" as the third point.

5. Do *you rely on a parent or other family member to fill you in on* *news about the rest of the family?*
If you find yourself calling up your mother and saying, "So, Mom, how are Jack and Sue and Bill? How's Dad? No—he doesn't have to come to the phone, that's all right," you're effectively keeping your mother in a position of power. How does this relate to triangulating? When you elevate one member of your family to matriarchal or patriarchal status and continue to relate to that member as the "clearing house" or "power source" of the family, it is probable that your psychic life is profoundly affected by this person in every way, and highly improbable that you'll ever get into a relationship without feeling the effects of that matriarch or patriarch. The family's "ruler" more than likely occupies a large space not only in the family, but in your subconscious mind—not to mention every relationship you get into.

6. Do *you usually wait until your back is against a wall before you* *make a decision?*
If "crises" tend to be your only real motivation for change, you're undoubtedly responding to a deep fear whose roots go back to your family. The fear of retaliation from siblings or parents that you feel unconsciously—the fear of what you project will be the "rage" that we've already discussed in our first and third questions—can become a terrible obstacle in decision-making later in life. It also generally makes a mess of any love relationship you subsequently get into. Whether it's choosing one partner over another or choosing to stay with a partner once you've gotten into the relationship, waiting for a "crisis" to decide your fate for you always spells disaster. And when you feel stymied to this degree by the prospect of making any decision, it's probable that there's a raging "third force"—a member of your family—at the root.

It may seem from all this that the Members of the Family Triangle has a lot in common with the Phantom Lover

Triangle—that the family member who makes up the third point of the triangle doesn't have to be "present" to hold sway in your life. This is true—although most Members of the Family Triangles do involve an ongoing relationship today with a sibling, parent, or other relative, often *reinforced*, as I suggested before, by the fact that this person may be in your root triangle, too. In other words, the brother who figures in your life right now may have been an important member of the root triangle that made your current relationship dynamics what they are. This means that you're continually relating to your relatives on two levels—that of today's relationship, and that of the strong past relationship which influences the way things are today.

Hooked by the past and the present to the family member (or members) in your triangle, you naturally find this triangle very potent. And one of its most potent and damaging effects has to do with the idea of *boundaries*. When you're caught up in a Members of the Family Triangle, it's hard to know how much information, guilt, responsibility, "love," or devotion you "owe"—and how much you're giving (or avoiding) out of reflex. Family members have special status in our lives: we often allow them to "barge in" in ways we'd never tolerate from friends. Parents may still act as if they "own" us; we may all but invite them to trample into our lives simply because we never realized we had the right to do otherwise. We may still react to our siblings the way we did when we were children, from abject adoration of an older brother or sister to fierce resentment of the sibling who "always got away with everything." All of this amounts to what one client of mine calls "boundary barging": allowing family members to intrude into your life beyond the appropriate boundaries of your respective roles. This limits your growth, which in turn impedes your ability to be freely intimate with your primary love partner.

Let's take a closer look at this dilemma, through some stories which make it clear that you *can* set boundaries even with your closest family members—and that in fact you must set them to have any chance of getting out from under the very stifling threesome of a Members of the Family Triangle.

▲

BOUNDARY BARGING

When Caroline learned that her brother Frank had been in a serious car accident, she panicked—she hadn't been in touch with him in years, and the prospect of possibly losing him filled her with dread, a dread that she didn't quite understand and whose force surprised her. She had always known that something between them wasn't "settled" yet. On the rare occasions she mentioned Frank in her sessions with me, memories of him seemed to plunge her into conflict: she obviously had ambivalent feelings about her brother that she had never allowed herself to acknowledge fully. But now that there was the risk of his dying, she rushed to his bedside, realizing that "something" had to happen, and be healed, between them—something she knew deep down they both had to confront.

This feeling of ambivalence and urgency about making contact with her brother had its roots in something very specific— something Caroline had been terrified to acknowledge in herself. She finally told me what it was.

"Frank was always a bully with me. I hated him when I was a little girl." Caroline stopped for a moment, as if embarrassed. It was obviously hard for Caroline to decide to continue, but she did, in a quiet, determined voice. "I promised myself I'd tell you everything, so here goes," she began. "When I was about nine," Caroline said, "and Frank was twelve, he made me touch his genitals. I felt terribly ashamed, but he took my hand and forced me to touch him, and then threatened me so that I'd be sure not to tell our mother and father. He was always violent," Caroline said, "always getting into fights at school and rebelling against Mom and Dad, and I was really frightened of him." Caroline said

said she kept away from him after this, and went to great pains not to talk to Frank throughout their teens unless she absolutely had to. Frank never again tried to force sexual contact with her, but she knew he felt that he'd gotten control of her—that he was the dominant child in the family. "It was as if all he wanted to do was prove some point," Caroline says. "He wanted to show me he could get me to do what *he* wanted."

Their parents, it turned out, were polarized about their children. The mother—a loud, overweight, complaining woman who had never had a kind word for Caroline—adored Frank, making excuses for him when he got into trouble, defending him at all costs. The father—a mild, somewhat ineffectual and henpecked man—adored Caroline, but couldn't abide his son. It was clear that the family had divided into enemy camps—and it was equally clear that the mother and father, who didn't get along with each other, had transferred affection and attention to the child of the opposite sex. There was, in other words, a *great* deal of subliminal seduction going on in Caroline's household.

In her current life, Caroline was married to a man with a quick, volatile temper, a man who sometimes even hit her when he was angry enough. Caroline had in fact first come to me because of problems with that relationship; Frank hadn't figured in her story much at all until she learned of his accident. When I suggested that there might be some connection between the abuse she experienced from her brother and the abuse she sometimes experienced from her husband, the idea of a triangle did finally begin to dawn for Caroline:

Caroline

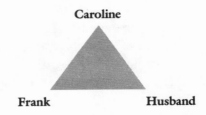

Frank   **Husband**

But what feelings did each of them call up for her? Caroline followed our triangle exercise and came up with the following lists of her feelings about all three triangle members to see what roles they might suggest. She wrote:

I feel that:

Caroline is	Frank is	My husband is
frightened	abusive	unpredictable
alone	cruel	insensitive
unfairly treated	dangerous	dangerous
unprotected	cold	unreliable

Caroline was amazed at how vituperative her descriptions were of both husband and brother—and she saw *each* of them as "dangerous." She never realized she harbored such negative, fearful thoughts about both of them, especially about her brother, so many years later. When I asked her to decide on the feeling themes they each exemplified in the triangle and label the triangle's respective points accordingly, she came up with the following:

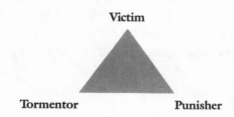

Victim

Tormentor   Punisher

"God," Caroline said as she saw that she'd labeled her husband as "punisher," her brother as "tormentor," and herself as "victim." "It sounds as if I'm living in hell! Where did I get these feelings?" That was exactly the question she needed to answer—and, after some thought, she was able to *see* where, as she labeled a third triangle with the first people in her life these themes brought to mind:

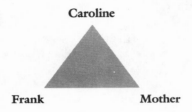

Caroline wasn't surprised to see her brother in her root triangle—but her *mother*, too? Then Caroline realized that although her father "loved" her, he wasn't able to protect her from her brother and mother, and she always felt unsafe. She also felt guilty—she knew she was "supposed" to love and be loved by her brother and mother, and she felt it was her fault that she couldn't. Marrying an abusive man meant giving her a second chance to win over a "difficult" person, the way little Caroline had tried to win over her mother's love and ease her brother's obvious hostility toward her. But because she felt "guilty" for not being a "good girl" and loving her brother and mother, and (on top of this) for having done something "dirty" with Frank, it also made sure she'd get "punished" as she unconsciously believed she deserved to be.

Fortunately, Frank recovered, and gave Caroline the opportunity to explore—and heal—some of the painful wounds that afflicted her. She hadn't seen Frank in years and didn't know that he had his own ambivalences about his childhood and his own painful memories. She was eventually able to persuade him to do the triangle exercises she'd done, and they both found some surprises. Frank was married to a woman who nagged him for not being successful enough—and when he understood the concept of a Members of the Family Triangle, he came up with the following three diagrams:

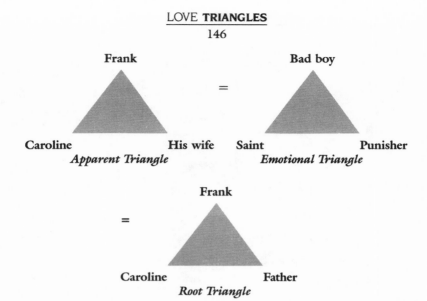

Frank

Caroline   His wife
Apparent Triangle

=

Bad boy

Saint   Punisher
Emotional Triangle

Frank

=

Caroline   Father
Root Triangle

Frank and Caroline began to understand that both of them had felt "plagued" by the parent who didn't express love to them in childhood, and both had perpetuated a pattern in their current lives that precisely reflected how that lack of love made them feel about themselves. Frank's feelings were further exacerbated by the fact that although he had the love and support of his mother, he didn't especially *like* her, and privately he understood why his father had turned against her and toward Caroline: he too saw his mother as an unattractive, complaining woman, and he felt he got "second-best." Now that he realizes that he was jealous of his father—who "got" the nicer, prettier female in the family—acting out sexually with his sister is suddenly all too understandable. However, because he felt so guilty about abusing his sister and his parents (through the ever-present subliminal threat of violence), he very carefully chose a wife who would make him feel as unworthy as he secretly believed himself to be. Since his sister wouldn't punish him, he unconsciously cast about for a woman who *would*.

When siblings allow themselves to actually listen to each other the way Frank and Caroline are learning to do, the flood of healing can be immense, because the compassion each learns to feel about each other's perceived "raw deal" can be profound. Now that their feelings and relationships have been charted in triangles, they can begin the second crucial "therapy" step of intimate listening, exploring fears and resentments and doubts they found too highly charged to face before.

Frank and Caroline need to do some "intimate listening" not only with each other, however, but with their respective spouses, too. While there's no guarantee that such intimate listening will "save" their marriages—it may become clear to all members that their relationships were ill-founded, and may be best served by leaving each other—the only way Caroline and Frank have a chance of restructuring their love lives satisfyingly is to face what's really going on beneath the reflexive behavior that traps them now. And, of course, there's no reason their spouses can't do the three-triangle exercise themselves to explore their own triangular attachments; Frank's wife and Caroline's husband will undoubtedly experience their own revelations about why they feel and behave the way they do. The net result will not only be increased clarity, but an increased chance of relating to their love partners with new respect and insight.

The "boundary barging" that Caroline and Frank experienced growing up—from the inappropriate seductiveness of their parents to Frank's abuse of Caroline when she was a girl—has had, each of them now realizes, a profound impact on their lives today. When you're not sure what the "rules" are in your family, you feel unsafe, and you quite naturally seek to defend or protect your self's boundaries from assault, either by responding belligerently (as Frank did) or through avoidance and running away (as Caroline did, by breaking off contact with Frank).

But you can respond in other ways that keep you locked into

difficult Members of the Family Triangle patterns, too. One of the most damaging triangular ruts we get into has to do with competing for love and attention, which many of us felt compelled to do from earliest childhood. Let's take a look at how two sisters learned to deal with this dilemma and get out of the triangles it got them into.

▲
THE COMPETITION RUT

Abby was the star of her family—she got straight *A*s throughout high school and captained the cheerleader squad and girl's hockey team—and she continued to succeed dazzlingly at one of the most prestigious "Seven Sisters" school in the country. Now, at thirty-five, she is a successful businesswoman, looks terrific, has a wonderful apartment in New York—in short, she's remained the envy of her friends. Except in one regard. She's never been able to hook up with a man her friends think is "worthy" of her. Even Abby admits that she doesn't understand why she keeps ending up with losers—perennially out of work, alcoholic, or still tied to their mothers. Abby has run the gamut of male "lost souls," and her love life is always a shambles. "How can I be so successful in the rest of my life and so bad at love?" was the question that brought her to therapy.

Abby's childhood seemed, on the face of it, "happy": her parents were supportive of her; they praised her for her numerous successes. But they were always distant about it. "It was as if I could never get much more than a 'That's very nice, dear, we're so proud of you' out of them. Although, God knows, I kept trying." But Abby couldn't see how her current problems with men related in any way to her disappointment with her distant parents. Or with her admittedly not very close relationship with her younger sister, Theresa. It was true she never really got along with her sister, but that was minor. . . .

A "triangle alarm" rang in me when I saw what short shrift

she'd given to her sister, so I asked Abby to tell me more about her. Theresa is three years younger than Abby, and it was clear that Abby was an awfully hard act for her to follow. "Come to think of it," Abby said, "I guess I did feel a little guilty about it. I mean, it wasn't my fault I'd done so well, but Theresa and I were close enough in age that she had all the teachers I'd had, not too long after I'd had them, and she just didn't do very well in school. I know she got compared to me all the time. It must have been hard for her." But Abby got immediately defensive (another "triangle alarm" to me): "What was I supposed to do? I mean, I tried not to flaunt my success in front of Theresa, but I was proud of my ambition. Theresa never seemed to have any."

Abby remembered one particularly painful moment. Theresa was in the seventh grade and she'd brought home her report card—and hid it for a few days from their parents. "I remember her tapping on my door," Abby said, "and when I opened it, I saw she'd been crying. Suddenly it all came out. 'How can I tell Mom and Dad I failed math?' she said. 'I'm just not as good as you, I can't help it.' She was so—pathetic. But it made me angry. I wasn't going to feel guilty. I told her she should just study harder, and closed the door." Abby sighed. "I've always felt guilty about that. But Theresa just makes me uncomfortable. Ever since, I've just never felt we were on the same wavelength."

Abby looked frankly miserable for a moment, then continued, "Of course, it didn't help that Mom and Dad seemed to *shower* her with attention—as if she were the poor little match girl or something. Here I was working so hard and Theresa wasn't doing anything—and my parents, pretty clearly it seems to me, picked Theresa over me. She was always the baby in the family. She still is now, as far as that goes."

There was no doubt in my mind that Abby had uncovered some strong "triangular forces" in her life. When I suggested that she was in a triangle, she was at first incredulous—but then began to take to the idea. At my suggestion, she began our three-triangle exercise and came up with the following:

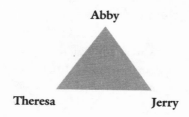

Abby

Theresa   Jerry

Jerry, the man she was involved with now, was another of the typical "losers" she seemed to keep ending up with—he'd just gone bankrupt in a small business he'd tried to get off the ground, and he was now going through various group therapies to "find himself." He also appeared to be living on dinners Abby paid for on their dates together.

Abby's "feelings lists" about herself, Theresa, and Jerry—which she accepted as her current apparent triangle—follow:

I feel that:

Abby is	Jerry is	Theresa is
pressured	self-absorbed	weak
resentful	ineffectual	incompetent
exhausted	unreliable	burdensome
lonely	distant	helpless

Abby's Jerry and Theresa lists stunned her. She had never realized that she'd continued to harbor such strong resentments about Theresa, and she suddenly saw that Jerry was a stand-in for her parents—something she'd never anticipated. Her emotional and root triangles, however, made this very clear:

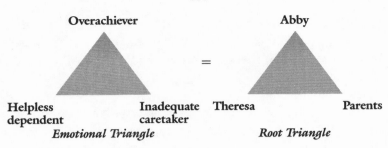

Overachiever · Abby

Helpless · Inadequate · Theresa · Parents
dependent · caretaker
Emotional Triangle · *Root Triangle*

What Abby realized is that although her parents were "supportive" of her as she was growing up, she never felt really protected by them—her successes always made her feel like an outsider. She saw that her attempts to be a superachiever were attempts to "outdo" her sister so that Abby would be the "favorite." But when she saw that Theresa, who wasn't nearly as competent as Abby, got more attention than Abby got, Abby was deeply resentful: here she was knocking herself out to please her parents and Theresa seemed to get all the attention without doing anything!

However, Abby also felt deeply guilty about overshadowing her sister. And so her attraction to "losers" was a kind of psychic penance: attempting to make it up to them was, in a sense, making it up to Theresa, whom she had shut out so often in childhood.

Simply coming up with these three triangles was healing to Abby—but she realized that she had to open up communication with Theresa, too. Members of the Family Triangles often afford you an extraordinary opportunity: you're often able to speak with crucial members of your root *and* apparent triangles today and heal old wounds. While it's true you can't go back and change the past, it can be wonderfully healing to find a new, empathetic connection with the actual person with whom you went through that past. As I've said, we respond on two levels to parents and siblings, and attempting to bridge gaps with those family members today can have a wonderful effect: the "past" can be healed, too, through understanding.

This was especially the case in another story, about a mother and daughter whose attachment to each other prevented them from relating to romantic partners in their lives. Jeanne, twenty-five, is Catherine's daughter—Catherine was only nineteen when she had Jeanne, and Jeanne says her mother admits she married too early. She broke up with her husband shortly after Jeanne's birth and ended up bringing her daughter up alone. It was a hard life, but a bond was forged between them that sustained Catherine—Jeanne says her mother confided in her as a sister rather than treating her as a daughter. Catherine was devastated when Jeanne, at twenty-two, decided to move across the country to the East Coast. "It was as if the bottom had fallen out of her life," Jeanne said. "We'd lived with each other for so long—and now suddenly I left. I knew it was hard for Mom—but, God, it was wonderful for me, at least at first. It was as if a heavy load had lifted. For the first time in my life, I was *free*." Catherine did, however, call Jeanne every day, sometimes staying on the phone for an hour or more. She worried about her daughter constantly.

Jeanne admitted that her lack of professional and romantic success didn't inspire much confidence: she lived in New York, where she was trying to find work as an actress, but worked more often in office temp jobs. She also found herself getting involved in a number of affairs. "It was great to get involved with men without my mother breathing down my neck," she said, "but I never met anyone I really *liked*." While these affairs were sometimes sexually fulfilling, they didn't touch Jeanne emotionally. "I kept wondering, Who *is* this guy? with every man I'd meet. I couldn't seem to hook up with any man who didn't seem

like a stranger." Then, Jeanne told me, turning a little white at
the memory, her mother came to visit.

Catherine was appalled. Jeanne was living in a ratty little apartment in the East Village, and it was obvious from the men's clothes
in the closet that she wasn't living alone. Mother and daughter
almost came to blows when Catherine insisted that Jeanne return
to California with her. Terrible ultimatums—"I'll never speak to
you again if you don't . . ."—were hurled back and forth.

Catherine returned to the West Coast, embittered and
depressed—exactly the way Jeanne now felt. Jeanne was so miserable, in fact, that she came for therapy. "Why do I let my
mother upset me so much?" and "Why can't I find a good relationship with a man?" were the two most urgent questions she
brought to me. I saw that our triangle exercises might help her,
and Jeanne was willing to do them. She came up with the following apparent triangle, the third point filled in, at the moment,
with a man named Mark with whom she was having her most
recent "affair"—a man who didn't inspire her emotionally any
more than any previous man in her life had:

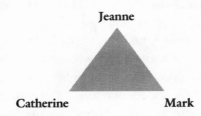

Jeanne

Catherine   Mark

Jeanne's "feelings lists" ran as follows:

I feel that:

Jeanne is	Catherine is	Mark is
depressed	smothering	unimportant
unappreciated	headstrong	kind but bland
angry	needy	unhelpful
achingly lonely	insensitive	undependable

Jeanne's eyes widened after she translated this into an emotional triangle:

Anxious caretaker

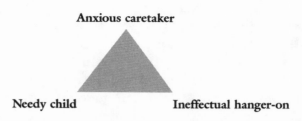

Needy child　　　　　　**Ineffectual hanger-on**

Jeanne was so stunned because she instantly realized who had first played those roles in her life, as she drew her third, root triangle:

Jeanne

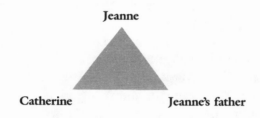

Catherine　　　　　　**Jeanne's father**

Jeanne suddenly realized she had always cast her mother in the role of "needy child"—never feeling that she could rely on her as a *mother.* "I was always taking care of my mother, listening to her confiding in me about what a bastard Dad was, as soon as I could," Jeanne said. "My mother always treated me as a confidante—someone she depended on for help." She was resentful at this, and yet felt guilty about expressing this resentment—hence "anxious caretaker." Her father had evidently been an alcoholic who couldn't keep a job and whom her mother had had to support, until she left him: an understandable model for "ineffectual hanger-on." Jeanne had to confront that she had pigeonholed men as "unimportant" and "undependable hangers-on" because her father had conditioned her to do so. Her three triangles opened up a whole new understanding for her.

Luckily, she was able to persuade her mother, Catherine, to view her own current life in the same triangular ways—now that they weren't rushing at each other with accusations, threats, and abject pleas, as they had when they'd last been together. When Catherine visited her daughter again in New York, she was able to come with her to therapy to explore how to make their relationship work better today. A significant dividend for Jeanne is that she is learning to let go of the feeling that she has to take care of her mother. She's also starting to see men as more than stand-ins for her absentee father. She now sees what patterns she had been in the grip of, and is starting to appreciate that she doesn't have to perpetuate them.

▲

DIAGNOSIS: DETERMINING YOUR MEMBERS OF THE FAMILY TRIANGLE

Simply by reading this chapter, you probably have gained a strong idea or two about what member of your family is taking unwanted space in your life, your relationships, and your mind. But in case you're still not clear about the third family point of your triangle and yet still strongly suspect that you're _in_ a Members of the Family Triangle, ask yourself the following questions to help you clarify who, exactly, that third point is. Put the answers in your journal so that you can reread your responses, perhaps to further develop them even six months later as you gain new insights.

When you get into an argument with your partner:

▲ Who in your family do you immediately wish you could talk to?

▲ Who in your family does your partner remind you of?

▲ Who in your family do you feel _your_ behavior is most like?

When you fantasize romantically about someone:

▲ Do you worry if a family member would approve? Whose approval are you most concerned with?

▲ Does your romantic fantasy remind you of anyone in your family? Who?

These questions should help you identify who the strongest family member prospects are in your triangle. You may find, in considering them, that you have more than one Family Member Triangle, depending on the situation or difficulty you're facing with your partner. You may find it helpful to map out more than one apparent triangle and follow each of them through via our usual steps:

1. Draw your apparent triangle.
2. List your feelings:

I feel that:

I am   **Partner is**   **Family member is**

3. Consider the list of possible feeling themes we set out in chapter 4 (page 59) to see, on the basis of the feelings you've just listed, which theme applies most strongly to each of the triangle's members. (Again, come up with any feeling themes that occur to you but that we may not already have listed.)

4. Reflect on who those roles remind you of most strongly from your past to come up with your root triangle.

▲

TREATMENT: HOW TO END BOUNDARY BARGING—CALLING "TIME OUT" WITH YOUR FAMILY

You may be able to accept in the abstract that you don't have to put up with "abuse" from your family. Especially when the abuse is obvious—your mother's haranguing you on the phone, your brother's barging in unannounced because he happens to be in town, your father's rude disapproval of your lover, your sister's assumption that you'll drop everything at once and come to her aid whenever she wants you to—you certainly have a clear idea of what's causing your resentment and that it's "unfair."

However, we are so insidiously tied to our families that we sometimes don't recognize "abuse" when it's happening—or, even if we do, we often respond in ways that increase tension between us rather than ease it, thereby strengthening the damaging "tie" that keeps getting us into trouble in the first place.

Here are some questions to ask yourself when you feel put upon by a family member—questions that will help you to gain the detachment you need to keep from rising to the same old bait. Take the time you need to write down your responses in your journal. Give yourself a chance to reflect on what you have said.

▲ Am I behaving with this family member the way I'd behave with a friend?

▲ Would I accept the behavior of this family member from a friend?

▲ Am I showing the courtesy to this family member that I would show to anyone who is not in my family?

▲ Am I being treated as courteously as I believe I have a right to be treated by anyone, family or not?

These four simple questions suggest guidelines—*boundaries*—that you need not only to set for yourself, but to be conscious of especially when you're in communication with your family. If you find that your behavior is worse with a family member than it would be with a friend, you have the choice to stop that behavior—to step back for a moment, assess what you're doing, and then change course, apologizing if necessary (just as you'd apologize to a friend if you overstepped boundaries with him or her).

If you discover that your family member is behaving inappropriately with you—that is, behaving in ways you would find unacceptable from a friend—you have the right, again, to step back and say, "You're hurting me," or "I don't think this is appropriate," or "Let's take some time out and talk to each other when we feel we can be civil." These suggestions may sound a little stilted—certainly their tone is not that which you normally employ with your family—but that may be a big part of the problem. The tone you allow yourself to use with family members may be part of the unhealthy "glue" that keeps you too tightly bound to damaging behavior with them. The main point is, you have the right to be treated humanely by *everyone*— including your family. And they have the right to be treated humanely by you. Simply stepping back for a moment to see if what's going on between you *is* "humane" is often enough to keep from falling into some terrible ruts—ruts that plunge you right back into old triangular habits.

Are there ways to elicit your primary partner's help in this whole process? Yes. When you feel the intrusion of yet another family crisis, whether a family member is actually on your doorstep or you know that you're reacting *as if* he or she were actually present, don't use it as an excuse to isolate from your partner. Use your journal as the first point of contact, first "know thyself," and next address your significant other. Ask yourself two simple questions:

1. *Have I let my partner know that something about my family is upsetting me?*
Perhaps the best thing you can do to at least momentarily "exorcise" your family from your primary love relationship is simply to *tell* your partner how you're feeling. Don't keep it bottled up. Don't expect that your partner will somehow magically understand why you're upset—even if your mother "always does this" and you feel your partner "ought" to know what's bothering you. Simply because a problem is obvious to you doesn't mean it will be obvious to someone else. Share your feelings with your partner—let him or her in on what's blocking you.

2. Have I asked for help from my partner to deal with this "block"?
This follows from the previous question. When you can, enlist
your partner's aid in a particularly difficult family situation. If
your sister insists that you run to her aid, or your mother can't
understand why you won't spend next Tuesday with her, or the
evening you planned to spend home with your lover is suddenly
broken into by your grandparents who "just happened to be
passing by," ask for your partner's help in coming up with a solution. Families commonly want you to "take sides"—often
against the "outsider," the partner you've left the family to live
with. Reinforce the feeling of "family" you have with your current partner—let that grow into as strong a bond as the family
you've left. You can do this, again, by inviting your partner to
participate in finding solutions to the problems your childhood
family precipitates.

The result of doing this questioning, and of involving your
partner in your "time out" process, will be freeing in ways that
you may not anticipate. Not only will you experience a surge of
relief at the release you'll feel from old and damaging "family
ties," but you'll see your partner in a new light. He or she won't
be a pawn in a family chess game anymore. You'll be able to see
who your partner really is—perhaps for the first time. And you'll
be able to see what kind of relationship you both might be able
to grow into, untethered to any of your old family triangles.

9

THE SCAPEGOAT
TRIANGLE

EMEMBER WHEN I SAID AT THE
BEGINNING OF THIS BOOK THAT
THE THIRD POINT OF A TRIAN-
gle doesn't even have to be human? You'll find out what I
mean when we explore Scapegoat Triangles. Basically, a
Scapegoat Triangle involves two people, one or both of whom
indulge in an activity in order to escape intimacy with each
other. The *activity* (which one or both partners blame for preventing closeness; hence "scapegoat") becomes the third point
of the triangle. One common example of this is the husband
who, hooked to TV football games, turns his wife into a
"football widow." But a job, a hobby, a pet, or simply, a habit
of puttering around the house can all constitute some very
effective and intimacy-blocking triangle forces—activities that
can become the "scapegoat" for why you don't have the time
and energy to attend to each other.

As you'll see, sometimes the noblest of outward intentions can mask a Scapegoat Triangle. The spouse who says he or she "has" to spend hours working late; the partner who self-righteously defends his or her "right" to find fulfillment in a hobby, avocation, or activity—these and other similar protestations can hide what may turn out, on closer examination, to be a deep fear of intimacy.

This isn't to suggest that all togetherness-avoiding activity is bad. Sometimes an activity works as a *necessary* buffer against overattachment, and by engaging in the activity the partner can buy himself needed time to regroup and revitalize. (I'll talk about this beneficial "regrouping" in more detail a little later on.) It's only when the activity becomes a reflexive or "addictive" escape hatch that it turns a relationship into a Scapegoat Triangle. Finding the line between beneficial activity and habitual escape is part of our task—which you can start to accomplish simply by considering the following Scapegoat Triangle questions. Remember to write your answers in your personal journal to have a permanent record of where you are now. You can then have the opportunity to reflect and review in the future.

▲
THE SCAPEGOAT TRIANGLE QUIZ

1. Do you find yourself annoyed that your partner "loses" himself or herself in an activity?

2. Do you—or your partner—find that the household chores seem endless, and that as a result you can't seem to find time together?

3. Do you feel that "doing nothing" is the worst sin—that people should always be busy?

4. Given a choice, would you or your partner rather be at work or with each other?

5. Are you resentful of your partner's abilities or talents?

Let's take a look at how answering yes to these questions reveals a bent toward Scapegoat Triangles.

1. *Do you find yourself annoyed that your partner "loses" himself or herself in an activity?*

"When he gets down to his workbench in the basement," Marge says about her husband, Jack, "it's as if he's in another world. I could tell him in a reasonably loud voice that the roof just fell in, Iraq just dropped a bomb on Cleveland, or he just got a call from his dead grandmother, and he'd respond with a 'That's nice, dear'—from somewhere far in another galaxy. Sometimes it makes me so angry. Why is he never this absorbed in me—in our marriage?" It can be exasperating to see your partner display avid interest in an activity—to see him or her passionate about an interest or inanimate object in ways that never seem evident with you.

When Marge begins a sentence (as she often does) with "If it weren't for his damned tools . . ." she gives us a clear indication that she's in a Scapegoat Triangle. Much as Marge may want to blame the inanimate objects that so absorb her husband, they obviously aren't the real problem. The real problem has to do with the intimacy-avoiding tactics those tools have provided her husband—tactics we'll learn to understand and deal with as we go on.

2. *Do you—or your partner—find that the household chores seem endless, and that as a result you can't seem to find time together?*

Not all intimacy-avoiding tactics are as obvious or specific as Jack's absorption in his workbench. Sometimes these tactics involve the mindless "busy-ness" of puttering around the house, busily picking off nonexistent pieces of lint, rearranging papers and magazines, deciding suddenly that the silver tray *has* to be polished this minute, or any number of other household chore distractions one or the other of you feels "has" to be done "this instant." "Busy-ness" can be a very effective triangular force. You may think you're simply doing what "has to be done," but what you may really be doing is avoiding intimacy with your partner, or preventing yourself from fully experiencing your own feelings.

3. Do you feel that "doing nothing" is the worst sin—that people should always be busy?
"The devil plays with idle hands"—how many of us didn't hear a variation of this when we were children? If you've raised "being busy" to the status of a moral good, you've probably been conditioned to believe that "doing nothing" is terribly dangerous—simply "being" yourself means you can't help but get into "trouble." But the idea that simply being yourself is threatening also can't help but block your ability to be intimate with a partner: how could you possibly let anyone else see you simply "being" who you are?

Concentrating solely on keeping busy often masks a fear that we couldn't possibly be "acceptable" (or even likable, much less lovable) if we were to cease being busy and simply "be." And so we clutch onto whatever our "business" happens to be as a means of self-definition: "I do therefore I am." What this self-definition can also do, however, is block us from sharing our deepest feelings with the people we love. Because it ends up preventing full intimacy with others, our attachment to "being busy" can become a formidable triangular block.

4. Given a choice, would you or your partner rather be at work or with each other?
Again, you may have to pause before answering this question accurately. Like Pavlov's dog, we often reflexively react to this question: "Of *course* I [or your partner] would rather be at home than at work!" But is that really true?

What role does "career" play in your or your partner's life? Even if you say you hate it, do you find yourself working late and on weekends over and over again, even when you don't really need to? Does your partner drop whatever he or she is doing with you the moment a work-related crisis comes up—is it clear from your partner's actions, if not words, that work is more important to him or her than you are?

The general area of "work" gives many people a huge but often very subtle escape hatch. In no other area can we be more firmly convinced that we're "right" in heeding work demands over all others. Our very culture encourages us to put work above all else. In convincing ourselves that we have no "choice" but to drop "everything" (for example, your relationship with your lover or spouse) whenever Work calls, we're reinforcing very effective means to escape intimacy—"work" can very effectively cloak our *fear* of being with one other person. Which means it can create a classic Scapegoat Triangle.

5. *Are you envious of your partner's abilities or talents?*
One woman I know whose husband is a professional violinist hasn't been to one of his concerts in years—even though his talent was one of the main reasons she was attracted to him when she met him. Why does she take so little interest in his career now? At first she said she was bored—she'd heard him so many times. But when she went into therapy she realized she was really jealous—not only because he had an activity into which he poured so much passion and concentration and with which he felt she had to "compete," but because she had no comparable outlet herself. She began to realize that her initial attraction to his talent really masked her own desperate desire to have the same talent—she really wanted to do what he was doing.

Jealousy and showing resentment of somebody else's abilities often mask envy of those abilities—and the distinction between jealousy and envy is an important one. Jealousy means feeling and showing resentment or hostility toward someone because of something he or she has. Envy means wanting that something yourself—wanting to be like that person. Example: Your jealousy may cause you to *resent* another person because he or she has a good relationship, making you aware of your own dissatisfaction—you almost wish that person were not so well off. But you envy the person's relationship and ability to be charming and open and competent—you wish you had that ability and such a relationship yourself. Once we have identified the envy behind our resentment, envy can, in fact, end up being productive: it allows us to identify the qualities we wish we had ourselves, and therefore we can lay the groundwork to *developing* those qualities. Jealousy, however, is always unproductive: it locks us into a stance that gives us nowhere positive to go. It also produces an enormous obstacle to intimacy—making it one of our most formidable Scapegoat Triangle forces.

One thing to make clear immediately about all of these questions is that while answering yes to them that you may be "using" or perceiving an activity as a threat or an escape hatch (thus turning it into the third point of a Scapegoat Triangle), not *all* "escapist" activity is bad. As I've said, it can even be beneficial to resort to an enjoyable activity to avoid intimacy for a time—when you need to reestablish boundaries, when you don't feel you can manage an intense union with another human being. It is normal to want to be apart sometimes; it is, in fact, crucial to continuing intimacy to allow yourself and your partner to separate when you need to. The stories we'll explore about Scapegoat Triangles in a moment should make this especially clear. As you read about Andrew, his wife, Sue, and his new business; Sal, Louisa, and Louisa's passion for skiing; and Laura, Bill, and Bill's absorption in sports, you'll see various ways couples can discover their need to come together, part, and come together again, sometimes using a third activity as a scapegoat, but eventually learning to see it as a needed temporary resource.

▲

BLINDED BY THE GRIND: THE TRAP OF TRYING TO DO IT ALL YOURSELF

Andrew, a thirty-five-year-old man who was fed up with the "corporate life" and his own unsatisfyingly slow ascent up the corporate ladder, decided to throw caution to the winds several years ago and start his own video-résumé business. Sue, his wife, was thrilled at first—Andrew's determination to make it on his own lifted his spirits, and his enthusiasm was contagious. Sue hadn't worked in several years; she had taken time off to stay home with her two young children, now three and five, a boy and a girl. Andrew wanted to keep it that way: he'd always wanted to be able to support his family without Sue working, and he was determined that she not go back to work now.

Six months into the enterprise, things looked pretty bleak. Andrew wasn't able to drum up the business he hoped for, and was working around the clock attempting to come up with schemes to attract business. He set up a cot in his office, where he'd sometimes collapse from exhaustion after working all day, only to wake up at dawn and continue. When he did come home, he was sullen and withdrawn. He'd carp about any evidence that Sue had spent money—even on what Sue knew were necessities for the kids and the household. "I felt like a huge burden," Sue said, "but every time I suggested going back to work, Andrew gave me this terribly pained, angry look—it was as though if I went back to work, it would mean he'd failed. So he just threw himself back into the office, and I ended up living month after month basically alone. It was terrible."

It got terrible enough that Sue delivered an ultimatum: either they sit down and talk about what was going on, even go for counseling, or Sue didn't know if she could stay on. Andrew kept telling her it was only a matter of time before he "hit it big," but time was passing and their relationship was simply getting worse. Finally he agreed to come in for therapy—which is when we began to explore the triangles that bound both him and Sue.

Andrew was able to see that he was in a kind of triangle, whose third point was his business:

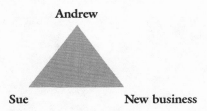

Andrew

Sue **New business**

When he listed the feelings that each member of that triangle elicited, he came up with the following:

I feel that:

Andrew is	Sue is	My business is
overworked	demanding	draining
not good enough	impatient	unpredictable
exhausted	doesn't understand me	full of problems
despairing	uncaring	unmanageable

What feeling themes did these feelings translate into? I asked Andrew to think, first, of himself and Sue—and then just to generalize about his business in a summary word or two. He came up with the following:

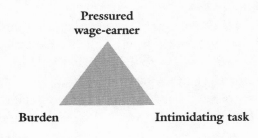

**Pressured
wage-earner**

Burden **Intimidating task**

When Andrew got to his root triangle, he quickly labeled himself in the "pressured wage-earner" slot—which was interesting, since it's evidently what he thought of himself not only as an adult, but also as a child. Had he really had to support his family back then? It seemed so—because the other two presences in his root triangle just as quickly occurred to him:

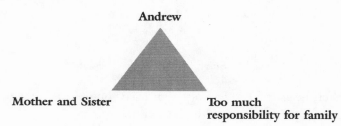

Andrew

Mother and Sister

**Too much
responsibility for family**

Andrew's feeling of "too much responsibility" as a child had a direct connection to his trying to be a superman in his new business today. Getting that business off the ground with no help, attempting to shoulder all the burden of his work and family alone, all reflected a pattern he felt from the age of nine, when business reversals led his father to suicide. Andrew felt he had to be the "man of the house" for his mother and sister. He also resented his father's death and felt that his father had taken the coward's way out of a stressful situation. His paper route and after-school work at a grocery store all helped to put food on their table: he ended up supporting his mother and sister, and they grew to depend on his support. It was what Andrew thought he "had" to be and do: take the reins of everyone's life around him.

Sue had her own complicitious triangle: a kind of Phantom Lover Triangle in which she was still directed by her father's voice today—a voice which told her that the "man" (in this case Andrew) had a right to "take over" her life, just as her father had taken over her and her mother's lives when she was a little girl. "What Daddy says goes" was her family's commandment, Sue said. "I guess I didn't have the courage to suggest to Andrew that I might be able to help him—and we ended up arguing about grocery bills when we might have given each other some comfort and understanding." Giving each other that comfort and understanding was something they learned to do as they tackled the "intimate-communication" exercises you'll read about in chapter 11; "checking" their urge to descend back into this Scapegoat Triangle is something they continue to do as they follow the exercises we'll come to in the "Treatment" section at the end of this chapter.

But let's just note one ultimate lesson they learned—a lesson we've been building to throughout this book, and will refine as we go on. Neither Sue nor Andrew could begin to confront what was going on in the Scapegoat Triangle that bound them until they could detach enough to see that they were in one— until they could become what I call "participant observers." They need to maintain their ability to observe the complexities of the relationship, with the intent in this case of blocking the reflexive urge to "blame each other" or Andrew's business for their trouble. Andrew and Sue's main goal, for which they both strive day-by-day, is to be participant observers, to see what they are doing while they are doing it. This isn't easy. It takes practice, but the rewards are considerable. It keeps them from blindly falling into the same old destructive triangular ruts. Being a participant observer means reminding yourself that you always have a choice, that you can choose not to act on the basis of what you observe or to passively let the same old habits prevail. This is freeing beyond anything that Sue or Andrew were once able to imagine. Later on I will give you pointers on how to enhance this ability. For now, at least, you are alerted to the direction you are headed.

Not all Scapegoat Triangles are evident all the time. The following one is seasonal, although no less devastating for cropping up only once a year.

▲

THE SEASONAL SCAPEGOAT TRIANGLE:
ANNUAL WITHDRAWALS

Louisa loves skiing and Sal loves Louisa. That, in any event, is how Sal, a thirty-two-year-old CPA, characterizes what goes on between them from late October to early April. Louisa has to agree: "I turn into an absolute ski bum every year," she says. "I can't help it—something about getting away, forgetting everything by speeding down those slopes, has become addictive. I wait all year for the few months I can take off for Vermont on weekends. And I want to share it with Sal—but he won't have any of it. He's never been athletic, and he's bored silly by the idea of spending every weekend in the snow. I miss him—but he knows how important skiing is to me, how important it is for me to get away."

Sal does know how important it is—and although he sometimes thinks he shouldn't make a big deal out of it, it makes him angry. "Louisa knows I'll never be a ski bum, and she's told me that it doesn't matter, that she loves me anyway. But why can't she spend even *one* winter weekend in town with me?" Sal simply feels that Louisa is on the verge of admitting, especially when he badgers her about it, that skiing is more important to her than Sal.

This wouldn't be such a big deal if their relationship were "casual." But they really do love each other, and they've been talking about getting married. The only thing is, Sal can't imagine what kind of wife—and, down the line, mother—Louisa would make if she wants to keep taking off on her own every weekend in the winter. He wonders if she's not only running *to* her rented ski house, but running *from* him and any hint of involvement with his adored daughters from his former marriage.

I knew it was important for Louisa to see how she had triangulated skiing—how she had made it a force in her life with which Sal felt he had to compete. And so I had her draw an apparent triangle, with skiing as its third point:

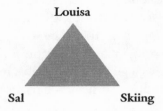

Louisa

Sal   **Skiing**

Then she drew up her "feelings list":

I feel that:

Louisa is	Sal is	Skiing is
pressured	self-absorbed	relief
freedom-loving	homebound	freedom
adventurous	cautious	fun
afraid of missing out on life	too family-oriented	salvation

More strongly than ever before, Louisa saw what an outlet skiing really was for her—how she depended on it, even *trusted* it more than she felt she could trust any human being, including Sal. When she condensed these feelings into feeling themes, this dynamic became even more clear:

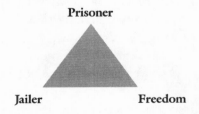

Prisoner

Jailer   **Freedom**

Again, the root of Louisa's skiing was an intense feeling—and as she began to transform her emotional triangle into her root triangle, she left no doubt about why she sped toward that feeling at every available opportunity. When she thought about her root triangle, she was flooded with memories. We'll investigate those memories in some detail in a moment, but the overwhelming feeling for Louisa was clear: she had wanted to "escape" ever since childhood. That urge to escape which was so strong in her today had been strong in her for as long as she could remember. Using that feeling as a guide, she was able to free-associate fairly quickly and come up with her root triangle:

Louisa

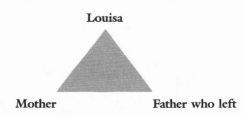

Mother   **Father who left**

That skiing was a stand-in for Louisa's father at first seemed surprising—but as she told me the story of her childhood it became clear why the two did equate. Her parents divorced when Louisa was only five. Her father left, rarely contacting little Louisa except for the occasional postcard or present—messages and gifts that usually arrived at Christmas, and usually had some "winter" connection. "My father even sent me a ski cap, now that I think of it," Louisa remembered. As a little girl, Louisa had imagined her father escaping to some wondrous wintery country in the Alps, where there were no restrictions such as she had to put up with, with her overworked, harried, strict mother. It was all too clear that skiing represented the freedom her father had found—and it was also clear that in some way, Louisa was taking off for the slopes every year in an unconscious desire to find her father.

Sal, of course, was left back in town with all the "responsibility"—responsibility Louisa felt guilty for not wanting to share, but which filled her with dread, because it was connected for her to the dreariness of her life growing up with her hardworking mother. Suddenly it was no wonder she fled at the first sign of winter for the slopes—and suddenly Sal began to have some empathy for how deeply rooted her urge to flee was.

This revelation was, as so many other revelations I've talked about in this book have proved to be, immensely healing to both of them. As well as practicing the intimate listening techniques we've been learning and will learn still more about later on, Sal and Louisa are now learning that Louisa's urge to flee *means* something more than either of them once thought it did. And they can take steps to reassure each other. Sal can let Louisa know that he never intended to trap her and that he will try to be more aware of what in his behavior makes her *feel* trapped; he also needs to look inside himself to see if some hidden part of him *would* in fact like to "clip her wings." Louisa, as she learns that responsibility doesn't have to be the onerous task she thought it was, can let Sal know she can be there for him without feeling threatened. Louisa will then see she doesn't have to resort to skiing to find freedom. There are other, more effective ways she can bring it into her life, all year long, ways, even, that she and Sal can share.

The real motives that Scapegoat Triangles can hide are almost always surprising. This is certainly true in our next story about what seemed to be the simple problem of a classic "sports widow."

▲

IF ONLY I WERE A FOOTBALL: THE PLIGHT OF A "SPORTS WIDOW"

Laura got engaged to Bill, she says, "despite the fact I knew he was a jock." She had no interest in sports, but she loved Bill for his earthiness, his direct approach to life, his easygoing nature. The problem was, he managed to *stay* "easygoing" only if he got his "fix" of sports on TV—or sports talk "with the guys." Bill once allowed Laura to come over on his "guys' night out" after she badgered him to let her join him, but Laura swears she'll never go through *that* again.

"All they do is grunt," she says, "which, when I was there, I correctly took to mean 'Get me a beer, lady.' They *live* in front of the TV, when they're not actually out playing sports themselves. Bill is a bit past his playing days, at least in the roughest sports, like football, but now he has company softball and squash. And there's *always* the damned TV. I feel as if the TV screen were a hypnotist—all Bill and his friends have to do is get within a half mile of the thing and they zoom in, locked for the rest of the day or night, or however long it takes the basketball, football, or baseball game to finish. Naturally they've got all the cable channels, which means there's never a lack of TV sports options. I feel as if Bill drops into the void every time he gets near the thing. How can I compete with all this?"

It was evident that Laura was in a powerful Scapegoat Triangle that she needed to look at. But she needed to see something a bit different from what made Bill get so sports-involved: she needed to see what her own complicity in the triangle was. Why was she attracted to someone like Bill? Why did she put up with it at all once she discovered the dynamics of Bill and his sports fixation? These were the uncomfortable—but necessary—questions her triangle diagrams forced her to face.

First she drew the obvious apparent triangle:

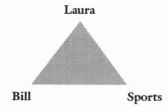

Laura

Bill   **Sports**

Then, when she drew up her feelings lists, she amazed herself at the vehemence with which she "attacked" the TV:

I feel that:

Laura is	Bill is	TV sports are
neglected	insensitive	brutal
lonely	self-absorbed	stupid
angry	weak	hateful
depressed	uncaring	demonic

"Demonic?" Laura asked, surprised at first by what she'd written about the TV. "But that *is* what I think. It's as if the TV were out to seduce Bill away from me—and he's too weak to resist it. I never realized what a malevolent force I think those TV sports are!" When she came up with the feeling themes her feelings made her think of, this hatred of what TV was "doing" to Bill and their relationship became all the more apparent:

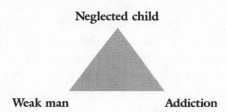

Neglected child

Weak man   Addiction

"Of course!" Laura said quietly, almost to herself. Then she explained her revelation to me: her father was an alcoholic. The original players in her root triangle quickly fell into place:

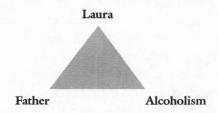

Laura

Father   Alcoholism

It was clear that, like many children of alcoholics, Laura had gravitated to a partner who had what seemed to her to be an addictive personality—certainly Bill's attention to sports and TV struck her as addictive. She had had a devastating childhood, never understanding how a bottle could be so much more important to her father than his own daughter. She now realized that she re-created the dynamics between her and her alcoholic father by choosing a man whose interests were patently far from her own, and whose involvement in those interests was as consuming as her father's involvement with booze had been.

Once she saw all this, she could step back from it and start to see that her "hatred" of the TV was misplaced. She realized she had many more options than she thought she had. She could begin to open herself up to sports, to try to understand what her husband loved about them; she could determine for herself whether his involvement was an intimacy-avoiding tactic or simply a genuine interest. She could take steps to *talk* to him about her own feelings about this involvement once she better understood his feelings about sports. She realized that she never tried to build a bridge to her husband; she only complained. Simply seeing how she had cast her husband in the role of her alcoholic father drew her up short: she knew that it wasn't only Bill who was being unfair—she was reacting inappropriately, too.

▲
DIAGNOSIS: DETERMINING YOUR SCAPEGOAT TRIANGLES

As with certain other triangles we've already seen, it's not always easy to define what the third presence in a Scapegoat Triangle is—especially if it's an activity *you* resort to in order to escape. (It may be all too obvious if you're a sports widow, however!) To determine whether you're *in* a "scapegoat activity," what the feelings are that it elicits and the roots of those feelings, ask yourself the following questions. Remember to write your answers in your journal, for review another time.

▲   When I'm upset, is there one activity I always want to do immediately? What is it? (Examples might range from cooking or eating to playing or watching sports, going to a movie, engaging in a hobby, working at your job or career—to drinking or taking drugs.)

▲ Being as honest as I can be with myself, would I always rather do this activity than be with my partner?

▲ Do I sometimes find that I continue to do this activity even when I don't enjoy it?

▲ What feelings does this activity bring to mind for me? (Examples might be relief, freedom, security, safety, warmth, fun, or just escape from boredom.)

Remember that you can turn these questions around and ask them about your partner too ("When my partner is upset, what activity does he want to do?" etc.).

But if you do find that you or your partner are hooked to a scapegoat activity, you'll have identified the third point of your triangle, and you can complete the three-triangle process you've already learned:

1. Draw your apparent triangle.

2. List your feelings about each presence in the triangle:

I feel that:

I am	**Partner is**	**Scapegoat is** **(or gives me)**

3. Translate those feelings into three feeling themes (again drawing for inspiration on the themes list on page 59) and draw your emotional triangle. Remember, however, that since the "scapegoat" isn't usually a person, you may want the role you assign to it to be the overriding *feeling* the activity gives you when you think of it (e.g., freedom, addiction, relief, intrusion, escape).

4. Draw your root triangle, labeling each point with whoever (or, in this case, sometimes *whatever*) most strongly comes to mind.

You now have what should be a revelatory series of Scapegoat Triangles. Reflect on what they say to you—and especially on how you may be reacting inappropriately to the presences in your apparent triangle now. Even before we get to the "Treatment" section of this chapter, new options and possibilities about changing your behavior may already occur to you simply as a result of looking at your triangle diagrams and how they interrelate—just as they have in other triangles you've explored in this book and, now, in your life.

But let's take a quick look at some techniques you can use to alter your behavior—and increase intimacy with your partner— that may not have occurred to you, and that are specifically geared to Scapegoat Triangulators.

▲

TREATMENT: FACING THE STUMBLING BLOCKS OF SCAPEGOATS

Unfortunately, the urge to "lose yourself" in an activity, or your partner's urge to do so, probably won't magically go away the moment you and your partner have charted all your triangles, understood their roots, and opened up a dialogue between you about facing what you're trying to avoid. As with every other triangular urge we've explored in this book, the Scapegoat Triangle urge is one to which we've been deeply conditioned to respond. As you'll have seen now in your emotional and root triangles, that urge didn't come from nowhere. You learned it as an adaptive survival tactic—and none of us gives up survival tactics easily, even if we can rationally see that their usefulness has long passed.

Let's focus now on what you can do to "hear" yourself when the old Scapegoat Triangle urge once again rears its head. When you want to "escape" and can think of resorting to nothing but the activity you know is your escape hatch, take a moment before you plunge into the activity to ask yourself some questions. Here again, your journal comes in very handy. Seriously process your answers by writing them down.

▲ What am I feeling? Am I anxious, frightened, angry, resentful, depressed?

▲ Do I really want to engage in my activity, or am I just trying to get away from what I'm feeling—am I really only after relief?

▲ If what I'm really after is "relief," are there other ways of achieving it than losing myself in my activity—ways that might give me an opportunity to sort out my feelings instead of hiding from them? What might they be? (Examples: lying down and giving yourself "quiet time" to meditate; calling a friend; sharing your anxiety or other negative feelings with your partner; taking a walk to change the scenery.)

The point about considering these questions is to remind you that you've got *choices*: that you don't *have* to "lose yourself" reflexively to escape pain or imagined danger. There are other alternatives. However, if your answers to these questions indicate that you're *not* desperately seeking "escape" through your activity but simply want to turn to it because you're passionate about it, you genuinely enjoy doing it, and it gives you the kind of nourishing "private time" you know you need, then, by all means, *affirm* your desire to engage in the activity: embrace it wholeheartedly, and go ahead and enjoy it. If your partner is upset by your involvement in this activity, try to open up communication. Encourage him or her to use the triangle-diagram method to understand the roots of his or her *own* stress about "losing" you to an activity. If, however, it becomes clear that you're allowing an activity to intrude on time you need to spend together, you may wish to rethink your use of time and arrange a schedule that affords an opportunity for the activity *and* spending time with your partner.

The main point in examining your involvement in an activity is to investigate your *motives* to see if you're approaching the activity in full, embracing consciousness, instead of making a reflexive attempt to escape something—or someone—that makes you uncomfortable. When you embrace an activity in this wholehearted way, it's no longer part of a damaging triangle—because it's no longer a block to intimacy. It's a tool you're using because you know it helps you to be all you want to be. When you're on that track, you feel no need for a "scapegoat." What's more, you find that you're more receptive to—and more capable of intimacy with—your partner.

10

THE HEALING TRIANGLE

NOT ALL TRIANGLES ARE DE-STRUCTIVE. SOME TRIANGLES CAN BE VERY BENEFICIAL IN-deed, giving you a chance to get a "second opinion," or simply to share something with someone else in a way that you can't with your primary partner. The triangle thus created is what I call a Healing Triangle—a triangular relationship that improves the quality of your life by enriching it, adding to it. As you'll see, what is added is often a healing *perspective*—a more spacious (and ultimately more helpful) view of the world than you're able to achieve with a primary partner alone, no matter how much you love or care about each other. It may also give you a nec-essary break at a time when a difficult situation or sudden crisis makes you especially hungry for more and different kinds of out-lets. A Healing Triangle never exploits or manipulates: it connects you in nurturing ways to each member of it.

The third presence that makes up a Healing Triangle might be a therapist—or it might be a friend or family member. While I've found in my own practice that it's extremely rare for a lover relationship outside the primary relationship to be anything but disruptive and destructive, sometimes it can be productive as a "cry for help": it can make clear what you need to address in your intimate life, and you can learn from it. (This kind of Lover Triangle is thus perhaps more accurately termed "instructive" rather than healing: we'll explore its dynamics in this chapter.)

Healing Triangles are beneficial for a simple reason: they take the pressure off a one-to-one relationship. The point isn't to enable one partner to "escape" the other out of fear of intimacy; rather it's to give that partner, and perhaps both partners, a little distance when distance is needed. The fact is, it's unrealistic to think you can get everything you need from one person—a notion society used to take heed of. It was once expected that we would talk things over with a clergyman, a doctor, or other "wise counsel" close to the family—someone, over the years, to whom you could turn when you needed another view you could trust.

Most of us no longer can depend on these outlets, particularly if we live in urban or semiurban localities—we move from job to job, house to house, relationship to relationship. With little feeling of permanence in our lives, we often lose the sense that it's even *possible* to have a second trusted confidant. (Often we're trying too hard to find and keep the first!) We're frequently not in one place long enough to develop this second resource—a resource we haven't, anyway, been conditioned to *want* in our lives. The modern romantic myth is "you and me against the world." Unfortunately, that myth can make the world of "you and me" awfully cramped. And the pressure this myth puts on our one-to-one relationships can be crushing.

Unwittingly or not, we often require of a love relationship something no one relationship could possibly do: to fulfill *every* aspect of ourselves entirely. When it inevitably doesn't (because it can't), our recourse is usually either to blame ourselves or our partner. However, the real problem is something completely different. What's wrong often turns out to be the *expectation* that we can get it all from one relationship. That assumption may be more damaging to a relationship than any other. It blinds you not only to what you *can* get from one other person, but to what you can get from other people as well, without jeopardizing the intimacy you want with your primary partner.

▲

REMEMBERING HEALING TRIANGLES
YOU'VE ALREADY HAD

You probably know more than you think you do about healing triangles. While you may now find yourself in the dilemma we've just described—expecting too much from one relationship—I'd be surprised if you didn't, at some point or points in your past, realize that you had to look elsewhere sometimes to fulfill certain of your needs. In fact, most of us learned to balance our needs between or among different people as children.

Ask yourself the following questions, and you'll probably prove this to yourself:

▲ When you were a child, did you have a "best friend"? Did you sometimes feel that your best friend could understand things about you your parents couldn't?

▲ Did you become especially fond of one or more teachers in elementary, junior high, or high school? Did you find yourself turning to that teacher for certain kinds of advice you didn't think you could get elsewhere?

▲ Did you have a favorite relative or adult family friend you always looked forward to seeing?

▲ Was there any authority as you were growing up you admired—perhaps a doctor or a clergyman?

What you were doing in any of the above cases was letting

someone other than your immediate family into your life—learning, in the process, that other people had important things to give and teach you. You were discovering the rewards of Healing Triangles.

Not all Healing Triangles in adulthood may strike you as so benign as the above childhood examples, however. Let's tackle what appears to be a much more dangerous case: the transitional triangle, when taking on a lover outside the primary relationship is at least temporarily productive because of what it can teach you about your needs. It's the most controversial of our Healing Triangles and needs some careful attention.

▲

THE HEALING LOVER TRIANGLE

First of all, as I said at the outset of this chapter, it's very rare to find a triangle involving a lover outside the primary relationship that *is* "healing." We've seen, especially in our chapter on destructive Lover Triangles, that this kind of three-way association can be extremely volatile and damaging—not only to the prospects of achieving intimacy in a primary relationship, but to positive feelings about each member's own *self*. This is primarily because when you turn to an outside lover, you've usually violated the trust placed in you by your partner, which makes you feel guilty. In most cases of "open marriage," the couple are looking for sexual diversity outside of their own union because some form of desired intimate risk-taking isn't happening in their union. Taking those risks outside the primary relationship, however, almost always spells trouble—and eventual disaster. Outside Lover Triangles (of the kind that "open marriages" can generate) are distancing tactics—and if you've seen anything in this book, you've seen that a triangle which is *set up* to distance you from intimacy is set up to lead you to misery.

However, sometimes—often at a time of crisis or when you come to an emotional roadblock that you can't seem to overcome in your primary relationship—you may turn to an outside relationship as a kind of cry for help. Sometimes your experience with the lover you've turned to can teach you something about the "help" you need, and the triangle, while still destructive, can provide at least relative "healing" if you're able to extricate yourself from it and make what you've learned the basis of new insight you can bring back to your primary relationship. Outside lover relationships usually leave scars, mainly because of the betrayal factor. You are either the one doing it or receiving it, and either way, no feeling is worse. But they can sometimes still be instructive in crucial ways. Look at Roger, Sharon, and Maria for an example of this kind of "instructive" Healing Triangle—and how, ultimately, it has helped each member of the triangle to grow.

Roger and Sharon, a reserved and quiet couple in their mid-thirties, had been married for ten years when Roger came to me for counseling. Their marriage was, he said, all but sexless. "I don't know what it was," Roger began, "but after about two years, sex sort of dissipated—it was as if we just couldn't muster up the kind of passion we needed to feel to *have* sex anymore." For a while, Roger said, this was all right—as long as they were having sex at least once a month. "Somehow our monthly love-making turned into a kind of ritual—even, I guess, a chore—which sort of re-inked the 'stamp' on our marriage, proved to us that we were still husband and wife." But as lovemaking became even more of a "chore," even this monthly sexual union started to disappear. A subtle but difficult tension had grown over the months and years—Roger and Sharon "accepted" each other without sex, but their emotional life cooled down to zero. "It's gotten to the point where it's as if we were roommates—except it's worse than that, because I know Sharon's not happy and she knows I'm not happy, and yet we never seem to be able to talk about it. I began to feel like maybe I *couldn't* make love anymore—not only to Sharon but to any woman. I felt like that, anyway, until I met Maria."

Roger had come to me now because he had just gotten into an affair with Maria, an Italian buyer who was temporarily in this country, working at the department store where Roger was working in sales and finance department. A business lunch date between them crackled with electricity: "It was as if I'd found a part of myself that had been buried for years and years. Maria and I clicked so completely that it was inevitable for us to become lovers."

Maria, according to Roger, was wonderfully liberating. "She lives for the moment," he said, "and she inspires me with the most incredible way of looking at the world—seeing the excitement again in things, seeing life as an adventure." Roger pointed out that he didn't feel drawn to Maria in the kind of deeper ways he still felt drawn to his wife. "My wife and I have years of understanding between us. What I have with Maria could never take the place of the relationship Sharon and I have built, the time we've taken to know each other." But Maria lit a spark in Roger's life that was nonetheless extraordinary, and, he had to admit, very welcome. All of his buried libido had burst back to life: "I feel I'm a *man* again!"

Maria was a divorced woman with two kids, and she had no illusions about marrying Roger. Neither, said Roger, did he particularly want to leave his wife for Maria. "I knew from the start that Maria would be in the United States for only a few months, and that was okay. I just want my life to be as good as this even *after* she's gone."

Interestingly, his life with Sharon began to change without, at first, his being fully aware of it. Rediscovering himself as a sexual being with Maria had awakened *all* of his sexual and romantic receptors—and made him want to approach Sharon in a different way. "Sharon knows that something is going on in my life," Roger said, "although I don't think she'd ever suspect I was having an affair. Not when I haven't shown interest in sex for so many years—I don't think it could have occurred to her. But now, well, we're starting to make love again. It's as if I've been so 'awakened' I almost can't help drawing her in." The problem was, Roger felt guilty. "I've always been monogamous before—and sometimes I'll fantasize about Maria when I'm with Sharon."

How was Sharon feeling about the renewed sex in their marriage? "She's never been warmer, and in some ways I've never felt closer to her," Roger said. "It's just that I can't help but feel like a sneak for two-timing her." Maria was due to go back to Italy in the next two weeks—a situation which Roger privately welcomed. "Now that I feel so different about myself, it's as if I don't need an outside lover. I'm starting to see ways of connecting with Sharon that will enrich our life together—not only sex, but emotional intimacy across the board."

Roger began to see, as he talked more about his improved sexual relationship with Sharon, that while his guilt was, in a sense, warranted—he *had*, after all, violated Sharon's trust in him—it didn't help to beat himself up with that guilt. Guilt arises whenever we feel we have violated a role boundary. Roger felt he had violated the boundary of his role of husband as established in Sharon's and his understanding of their marriage—which in fact he had. But Maria had also been a kind of *gift*—an answer to his cry for help, his need to be a sexual being. She had shown Roger that he was capable of initiating passion in a woman and had nurtured a kind of enthusiasm for life that was transforming Roger's view of everything—not only "love," but his whole approach to friends, coworkers, and family.

This is not to say there hasn't been damage. In fact, no one escaped this triangle unscathed, even Maria. She allowed herself to "use" Roger and be used by him. They turned sex into a kind of tennis match—a sport rather than a means of sharing the deepest parts of themselves. Roger felt guilty not only because he'd violated his wife's trust but because he knew he was, in a sense, misusing the passion Maria evoked in him. He needed to bring that passion into a deeper love relationship where it would have more meaning.

The upshot of this kind of an affair is not always the happy ending Roger found with his wife, Sharon. Sometimes such a relationship teaches you that your primary relationship really *isn't* adequate to your needs; occasionally the outside relationship may legitimately develop into a new primary relationship. And sometimes—often—when trust is violated in the way Roger knew it had been, it can be very difficult to build that trust up again with the same primary partner. Roger knew Sharon "sensed" something was going on—and often what the left-out spouse senses in a triangle is a subtle but definite distancing that can, if allowed to persist, badly erode the marriage.

So obviously, when we talk about a triangle like the one that involved Roger, Maria, and Sharon, we are on dangerous ground. Habitual triangulators are experts at denying their own motives, and I can't stress too much that most Lover Triangles fall into the first category we explored in chapter 5—the damaging, intimacy-avoiding category. More than this, I have never known a "positive" Healing Lover Triangle to be more than transitional, as in Roger's case; it was important that the self-confidence he gained with Maria become something he could bring back to enrich his primary relationship.

When triangles "heal," they do so because they enable you to see yourself and your behavior from a completely new vantage point. You know a triangle is healing when, after contact with the third presence in it, you feel refreshed and renewed, and thus more capable of an easy, open intimacy with the primary person in your life—of a more detached perspective that enables you to affirm and celebrate who each of you is. For obvious reasons, taking on a lover usually involves destructive "covert" tactics that, eventually, can't help but erode that sense of intimacy. Outside lover triangles may *teach*—but they're only "healing" if you're able to exit the affair and bring what you've learned back to the primary relationship.

But let's now look at some more general characteristics of

Healing Triangles that apply to all of them, especially the major-
ity of permanent Healing Triangles that don't involve outside
"affairs"—the Healing Triangles you're able to make an open part
of your life.

▲

LEARNING TO "SELF-CORRECT" THROUGH HEALING TRIANGLES

In his book *A Safe Place: Laying the Groundwork of Psychotherapy*,
Leston Havens, professor of psychiatry at Cambridge Hospital
at the Harvard Medical School, describes the triangulation tactics
of a woman who is one of his clients: "If she mentioned a boy-
friend, one of his past loves soon appeared. Discussion of mother
led to father. The pattern of her mental reflections was three-part,
seldom the patient and only one other person." *Aha*, I can hear
you say—the poor woman is caught in any number of triangle
traps.

Not according to what Professor Havens says next: "I have
come to trust this [three-part pattern] as a sign of basically sta-
bilized inner life. It has often been claimed that triangulation
means that patient's development has incorporated a secure family experience that anchors mental life."

Here is the flip side of the predominant view of triangles we
have developed so far in this book—and alternative view that is,
in fact, crucial. Far from always being damaging escape tactics,
triangles—that is,what we are calling Healing Triangles—can
work to bring *balance* to our lives. How? Triangulating can nurture, Havens says, "a self-correcting tendency": by thinking of,
or interacting with, the third presence in a Healing Triangle, we
can remind ourselves of *alternate* ways of seeing and dealing with
a situation. We can remind ourselves that the *one* way we've
started to look at something doesn't have to be the only way. This
is the essence of what Healing Triangles provide: the opportunity
to "self-correct"—to *realign* ourselves when we become overly

influenced by a single partner, by looking to another person to give us a different perspective, a "second opinion." Basically, healing triangles are beneficial because they allow you to separate in order to achieve a more detached perspective when a one-to-one relationship becomes too intense.

▲

DIGGING OUT OF A RUT: DAN AND MARILYN

One couple who come to me for counseling have had a particularly difficult time getting out of the rut of a relationship which had, in a sense, become *too* close and interdependent. At first meeting, Dan and Marilyn seem to most people like the perfect couple. Married for fifteen years, both in their late thirties, they are professionally successful: Dan is an investment banker and Marilyn is an advertising CEO. What's more, they both romantically assert that they "couldn't live without" the other. Every moment they spend out of the office they spend together. This means repairing to their isolated house in the Hamptons whenever they can get away from the city, or burrowing in on weekends in their Upper East Side penthouse apartment when they can't.

However, as I soon discovered, the key words were "burrowing" and "isolated." Dan and Marilyn had blocked everyone but each other out of their lives. And it turned out that their single-minded devotion to each other didn't entirely spell bliss.

They came to me for counseling (at Marilyn's insistence; Dan grumbled at the idea of letting even a therapist know about their problems) because they found themselves blowing up at each other for the most trivial reasons: Marilyn kept ordering takeout food Dan didn't like from the neighborhood gourmet shop; Dan kept dropping his socks outside the hamper; the toothpaste cap wasn't screwed on right; the window shades weren't pulled down at the right time. Their arguments, however "trivially" motivated, were becoming more frequent—sometimes even violent. It was clear that whatever one of them said or did always had a magnified effect on the other.

When your emotional world involves only you and one other person, distorted reactions are virtually inevitable. What Marilyn and Dan desperately needed was some space—an opportunity to detach from each other long enough to get a better sense of what was really going in their marriage, what it was that they each really wanted, felt they were missing. They needed to *listen* to each other in ways they hadn't so far learned or allowed.

Coming to a therapist was a good first step. In fact, therapists can play a very beneficial Healing Triangle role—they can "be" the clergymen, doctors, and other mentors society once encouraged us to cultivate for counseling. But Dan, especially, was very wary of letting me in, even as a "neutral" therapist. His root triangle revealed why.

Dan's father had died when Dan was a little boy, and he was plunged into the classic scenario of "You're the man of the house now"—he felt he had to take care of his mother forever after. He lived with her until the day he got married to Marilyn, and now his entire life, which once revolved around his mother, revolved around his wife. His root triangle was connected all too clearly to the triangle he was in today—a "phantom" triangle involving what Dan labeled "my father's ghost":

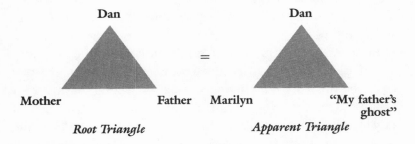

Dan	Dan
Mother Father	Marilyn "My father's ghost"
Root Triangle	*Apparent Triangle*

Throughout his boyhood, Dan had felt doomed to loneliness: not only didn't he have a father, he didn't have any friends. He was a self-described "loner"—quiet and studious at school, distant from his classmates—rushing home every day to "take care of" his mother. Unconsciously, he felt as if the only legacy from his father was to be saddled with the responsibility of devoting his life to *one* person. Since his mother, too, had died by now, all of his energies centered on his wife—which was just "fine" with Marilyn, whose own root triangle more than made her welcome Dan's desire to focus exclusively on her.

Marilyn's father had adored her and showered her with single-minded attention, making it very clear that he preferred his daughter to his wife. Marilyn's "victory" over her mother for her father's attention was not, however, a comfortable one: she shut her mother out of her life, but felt guilty about it—that she was the favored female in the family—and the guilt was reinforced by the real resentment she picked up from her mother because Marilyn had "stolen" her man away. Now Marilyn found she couldn't allow herself to "trust" anyone besides her husband. Not only did she block out her mother in her life today but also the possibility of intimacy with *anybody* outside her marriage.

However, despite their isolation tactics, both Dan and Marilyn actually *ached* for a feeling of being connected to a larger world—to other people. Then they tried something they'd never attempted before. In the safety of therapy, they began to talk about their buried desires to connect to the world in larger, more satisfying ways.

Because Dan felt he was so "sophisticated" about the "nonsense" of religion, he was embarrassed to admit that the one thing he missed from childhood was the feeling he got from going to church. "Not that I believed in God or anything," he quickly said, "but—well, all the *people* were so nice. It was the only feeling of camaraderie I guess I've ever known. I always felt good just sitting in the congregation with my mother. As if I'd found someplace I sort of belonged. Only 'sort of,' though. I mean, I couldn't buy all that religious stuff. But I felt safe there, even happy. . . ."

Marilyn made a similar confession. In college she had belonged to a debating society, and it was the only "group" she ever enjoyed going to. "I guess I never felt really accepted anywhere else," she said. "But I was good at debating. And the other girls—I went to one of the last diehard all-women schools in the Seven Sisters—looked up to me, admired me. I had fun there—I looked forward so much to our meetings, and to the competitions. I felt I was *part* of things, as if people really liked me."

Neither Dan nor Marilyn had experienced anything like this before or since: each had thought of himself or herself as a "loner," an "outsider," someone essentially isolated. The real message they were broadcasting to each other when they blew up during one of their "trivial" spats was simply that they were lonely for other companionship—they needed more outlets in their lives than they could provide themselves alone. They needed *other people*. They also needed to learn that it was normal— perfectly okay—to want this wider companionship, and that it didn't have to threaten their own close bond.

We'll find out what Dan and Marilyn learned about reassuring each other when we get to the "Treatment" section at the end of this chapter. But first, let's look at a few other people to see how they've managed to acknowledge their own needs for Healing Triangles and work them into their lives.

▲

THE "DIALECTIC" OF REACHING OUT FOR HELP

Sara is a working woman who identifies all too strongly with other women her age—mid-thirties—who worry about the "biological clock." Although she and her husband, Max, aren't quite in the financial shape she hoped they'd be in by the time she decided to have a baby, she now finds herself pushing for it anyway. "How much time do I really have?" she asks herself.

But she still feels torn—which is why she came to me for counseling. "I so much want to have a baby," she says. "Every time I pass a mother carrying an infant my heart aches—I want that mother to be me. And now I've gotten Max to agree. But— why am I still so frightened? Why can't I just go ahead and do it?" Sara kept a private calendar on which she wrote red checks on the days she wanted Max and her to "start conceiving"—but as those days approached, she'd cross out the check and postpone the date. She was terribly uncomfortable about confronting her real feelings. Her sexual relationship with Max had always been enjoyable—but now, more and more, she felt totally turned off. "It's not that I find Max repulsive or anything," she said. "It's just that the idea of making love—when it comes right down to it—always seems to be the *last* thing I want to do. I keep saying no to Max even on the days I've decided to say yes. I just can't seem to let myself have sex right now. At this rate, we'll never have a baby."

It was clear to me that Sara's ambivalence about having a baby was causing problems. She had built up the "conception dates" on her calendar to such a degree that they frightened her—planning abstractly "in the future" to have a baby and actually trying, right now at this moment, to *conceive* that baby were two very different things. It was also clear that Sara hadn't told anybody but me about her fears and doubts. "I can't discuss it with Max," she said. "Not after pushing him for so long to have this baby. He'll think I've lost my mind!" I asked her if there were anyone else she could talk to about this besides me. "Well—I guess I could call my sister, Rachel. We've always been pretty close. But she's had three kids already—she'll probably think I'm a baby myself for being scared. How could she understand?"

People who resist Healing Triangles are adept at projecting

exactly why no one could serve as a true confidant. When you dig down deep enough, you'll always be able to come up with an irremediable "reason" why even a close friend "could never understand." It takes courage to decide to try to reach out anyway. I sensed that Sara very much needed someone she could talk to, especially a woman who had gone through the decision to be a mother herself. I asked her what she thought was the worst thing her sister could say if Sara were to talk to her about her feelings. Sara thought for a moment. "She'd probably just tell me not to worry about it! I guess I can't imagine her saying anything worse than that." She paused, and said, "That doesn't sound so bad, does it? Maybe I will talk to her."

Letting her sister in turned out to be very helpful. Sara came back to me, wide-eyed. "I can't believe it! My sister—a mother with three kids—said she knew exactly what I was talking about!" Sara's sister, Rachel, evidently had gone through all sorts of agonizing doubts before deciding to have her first child—and the decision to have more children was no easier. The wonderful sense Sara had was that she wasn't alone in her own doubts and fears—and that feeling of "connection" freed her. "I'm starting to feel that I'll be able to handle whatever I decide, one day at a time. If my sister can do it, I can too."

What Sara has created for herself—and what any Healing Triangle creates—is a kind of dialectic. The dictionary defines dialectic as "logical argumentation"—which is exactly what Healing Triangles enable you to engage in. Sara could begin to weigh pros and cons of having a baby only when she allowed herself truly to *imagine* the pros and cons, not simply react reflexively out of fear to them. Talking to her sister helped her to do this. Finding someone who she felt truly understood drained much of the fear away and Sara was able to synthesize all of her emotions, and a more balanced weighing of pros and cons, into a decision she felt was realistic—a decision to have a baby which *took into account* her fears, told her it was perfectly normal to have those fears. She was able to synthesize a decision to have a baby with which she could feel comfortable.

There are three emotional parts to the "dialectic" she eventually afforded herself: what are called the "thesis," the "antithesis," and the "synthesis." These are the three essential stages all of the rest of us must go through before making peace with any decision, too. What do they mean and how do they work? Let's take Sara as an example to show you:

Thesis: The thesis is the presentation of the idea. In Sara's case, this simply meant: "I can't wait to have a baby."

Antithesis: The antithesis is the objection to the idea—its reverse. For Sara, this meant: "I don't want to have a baby—I'm too afraid."

Synthesis: The synthesis takes into account both the thesis and its opposite, the antithesis, and attempts to reconcile them. In Sara's case this meant: "I acknowledge I'm afraid, but I can see from other people's experience that I can handle that fear. I will go ahead and have the baby and try to be open about my feelings with people who understand as I go through the whole process."

Clearly, Rachel's input was essential in allowing Sara to reach her synthesis. So, for the rest of us, are Healing Triangles essential in helping us to achieve balance in our own decision-making. But what Sara's husband and her sister also were to her were "mirrors": they each reflected back certain aspects of herself more clearly than she could have seen those aspects on her own. The function of other people as "mirrors" in our lives is crucial to our self-definition. How does a baby know what the effects of his crying or laughter are without a mother to react to them? How do we know how we're coming across in the world until we see other people's reactions to our behavior?

Obviously, if you've only got one mirror you'll have a very limited view of yourself. And when that limited view is a negative one, it can have devastating consequences. Let's look at how we can begin to supplement our lives with these beneficial "second mirrors." I'll offer some concrete suggestions, again organized according to the two-part "Diagnosis" and "Treatment" program we've been using throughout this book.

▲

DIAGNOSIS: WORKING OUT YOUR PERSONAL "DIALECTIC"—ASSESSING YOUR NEED FOR A HEALING TRIANGLE

Remember what we said about the necessary "dialectic" each of us must engage in before we can come to peace with any decision we make in our lives? You can assess your need for that dialectic—and thus make way for a Healing Triangle—in the following way.

When you feel "trapped" in your relationship with your primary partner—when you feel emotions have gotten too intense, and that you're too close to be able to get any kind of detached perspective about what's going on between you—try this dialectic exercise. Record your thoughts in your journal.

1. *Find the thesis. State, as clearly as you can, what you want to happen.*
Be specific. Don't say, "I want my partner to understand me better." Say (as appropriate), "I want to be able to go out one night a week with my friends," or "I want us to go on a vacation this year," or "I want my parents to be able to visit us in September." What you're doing here isn't so much stating "the conflict" as stating what *you* want out of the conflict.
   Now ask yourself: "Who in my life supports what I want—is there anyone I can talk to who agrees with me?"

2. *Find the antithesis. State, as honestly as you can, your fears about*

what you want to happen or why you think you might be wrong in wanting it.

This doesn't mean simply stating what your primary partner thinks—unless he or she has articulated it the way you would. But again, be specific. And be honest. If you said, for example, that you wanted to take a night out away from your partner, examine your real fears and motives, and express them to yourself: "I really want to get out *every* night of the week because I just don't feel we're close anymore," or "I'm really trying to avoid telling my partner that I'm not happy with our lack of communication," or "I'm frightened of letting my partner see who I really am."

Now ask yourself: "Is there anyone in my life with whom I could talk this over?"

3. *Look for the synthesis. Imagine a decision that takes into account both sides of the problem and that you feel you can be most comfortable with. Make a pact with yourself to discuss the pros and cons with someone other than your primary partner.*

Do some balancing between your answers to questions 1 and 2: has the "antithesis" tempered the "thesis"—do you now see the problem in a new light? If, for example, you realize that your desire to spend an evening or more away from your partner is partly that you're trying to avoid intimacy with him or her but that it's also a genuine desire to have an evening to yourself, you might "synthesize" the following decision: "I will take one evening a week for myself, but I'll also do everything I can to increase intimacy in my marriage."

When I say "make a pact . . . to discuss the pros and cons with someone other than your primary partner," I'm moving out of "diagnosis" into "treatment." But part of our diagnosis is to find out at least preliminarily if there *is* anyone you feel you can talk to—someone who can afford you a Healing Triangle. Let's explore that a bit more right now.

▲

TREATMENT: FINDING THE "MIRRORS" YOU NEED TO SEE YOURSELF

We have already seen that we need other people. Their reactions to us indicate if we indeed come across as we intend to. They help us increasingly to define our own identity. Accepting this, it is obviously important that we look for constructive mirrors. And it's equally obvious that we can benefit from having more than one mirror in our lives.

Let's return to the questions I asked you to ask yourself in our "Diagnosis" section, which boil down to: "Is there anyone I can talk to about my feelings—other than my primary partner?"

On the left-hand side of a piece of paper, under the heading "Second Mirrors," begin a column—a list of people who come to mind when you ask yourself this question. Leave space between the names. Even if no one seems exactly "right" or especially appropriate as a confidant, don't let that keep you from writing the names down. Your list might run along the lines of the following:

Second Mirror

My neighbor Joyce

My hairdresser Mary

My ex-boyfriend John

My sister Karen

Now, on the right-hand side of the page, head another column with "Positive Traits," and then write down what draws you to each of these people—what makes you think they'd be good to talk to. It might run as follows:

Second Mirror	Positive Traits
Joyce	Pragmatic, down-to-earth, no-nonsense
Mary	Experienced, wise, innovative
John	Knows me well, cares about me
Karen	Understands me, has sense of humor, patient

Don't focus on the negative—which I know you'll be tempted to do. For now, just allow the inevitable "Yes, buts" to go past you ("Yes, but Joyce isn't as kind as she could be"; "Yes, but Mary doesn't really know me that well"; "Yes, but John is too biased to give me an objective opinion"; "Yes, but Karen hasn't gone through what I'm going through"). It's not that there might not be some truth to your "Yes, buts," but I don't want you to lose sight of what you *can* get from the "second mirrors" in your life—which concentrating on their "negative" traits will encourage you to do.

Now consider the "synthesis" you've come up with in our "Diagnosis" section—the decision you feel most comfortable with about whatever problem you're confronting. Who on your list would you feel most comfortable talking to about this synthesis—this decision? Who do you feel is most appropriate? Perhaps more than one person on the list seems like a good prospect. That's fine. There's nothing that says we have to limit ourselves to *one* Healing Triangle in our lives. You can have second and third and fourth and fifth mirrors, too—the third "point" in your Healing Triangle doesn't have to be filled by only one person.

Once you've identified one or more likely "third points," take the plunge. Pick up the phone right now. Make plans to get together. If it helps, concentrate on the positive traits you've just written down as you dial the number: remind yourself of the wider perspective—and the caring support—this person could give you. What you're doing is finding a "mirror" that will help you to *affirm* yourself and lead you to options you may never have considered, alternatives that may end up bringing you closer not only to your primary partner, but to other people who care about you as well.

The urge to isolate won't magically go away—not when you've been conditioned for so long to react reflexively by drawing back into yourself or clinging to your primary partner. To keep you on track once you've begun to allow Healing Triangles into your life, try the following quick realignment exercises when the urge to isolate hits again.

Three Ways to Keep from Sliding Back into the "One-on-One Rut"

1. Pick up the phone.
Just because you're not physically near any of your "second mirrors" doesn't mean you can't contact them—right now. Don't project that you're "imposing"; simply take the action and reach out. If one person isn't home, try another. If all you get is an answering machine, leave an honest message—say that you felt the need to talk to whomever you're calling, and perhaps give some indication of what the problem is. Don't cover up your need or pretend to be feeling something you aren't.

2. Be somebody else's "second mirror."
Offer to "be there" for someone else who you sense is isolated—and who looks as if he or she could benefit from a Healing Triangle. It's amazing how healing offering to listen to somebody else can be. Even if your own problem is obsessing you and seems insurmountable, you can get some surprising new perspective on it when you reach out to help somebody else.

3. *Turn to a group when you can't find an individual.*
You won't always be able to find an individual "second mirror."
But that doesn't mean you can't avail yourself of other people
options. Remember how even "sophisticated" Dan missed the
camaraderie he felt as a child in church? There's no reason why
you can't cultivate participation in a group. It might be a church
or synagogue, it might be a common-interest organization, it
might be a class in a subject you're interested in—it might even
be group therapy! Sometimes simply putting yourself in other
people's presence, even if you don't know them well individually,
can have a lightening Healing Triangle effect. And, of course,
those groups can be the source of *new* "secondary mirrors"—
you'll be giving yourself the opportunity to develop people skills
that will afford you the chance to tap into the resources a
Healing Triangle can offer.

R e p l a c i n g   " V e r s u s "   w i t h   " P l u s "

The kind of buoyancy and feeling of self-sufficiency Healing
Triangles can bring to your life is wonderful. You begin to get
a strong sense of yourself as an individual as well as someone
who desires closeness to your primary partner. This brings up
an important point. You can't achieve true satisfaction in life
without grappling with two essential needs: the need for intimacy and the need for "individuation"—self-definition.

But aren't these two essential needs contradictory? Isn't it
always a painful struggle to satisfy both of them?

It doesn't have to be. In fact, what we'll learn about next—
"intimate communication"—can replace the "versus" in that
equation with a "plus" sign. It can enable you to *accept* both
needs and orchestrate them into your life with your primary
partner. In our next chapter, we'll take one final—and very
specific—look at how we can best do that. It's what we've been
building toward throughout our triangle journey: how to find

satisfying intimacy with your partner without threatening or curtailing who either of you is. Healing Triangles begin to show us the way. But we can go a little farther along that road than we've traveled so far. The destination of affirming the bond you feel with your primary partner and affirming each of your selfhoods is more achievable, perhaps, than you ever dreamed.

11

REACHING THE GOAL

ACHIEVING TRUE INTIMACY

IF YOU'VE LEARNED ONE LESSON ABOUT DESTRUCTIVE TRIANGLES, IT'S THAT THEY KEEP YOU FROM EXPERIENCING true intimacy—and all of the rewards of true intimacy—in your one-to-one relationships. And if you've learned anything about *con*structive triangles (like the Healing Triangle), it isn't only that they can enhance the overall quality of your life, but that they enhance intimacy between you and your primary partner.

In all of the "Diagnosis" and "Treatment" sections in the preceding chapters, no matter what triangle they related to, my overriding goal has been to bring you closer to the moment when you can face your primary partner with your full, open, loving self. Our exercises have been designed, above all else, to help rid you of the crippling *fear* that assails so many of us when we face the prospect of opening our hearts and lives to another human being.

204

Triangulating, when it's destructive, always puts a wedge between you and the person in your life to whom you most want to express love. And now that you've discovered the reasons for your own dependence on triangles, it's no longer a secret why and how you learned to use the triangular wedge to distance yourself. At one or more distant points in your past, you learned that intimacy was unsafe. You learned that the only way you could protect yourself was to corral another third "buffer" presence to keep you from the "dangers" of full, head-on participation in a one-to-one relationship.

The exercises you've followed in this book have all brought you within hailing distance of this book's final goal. What is that goal? To help you *communicate* with your primary partner—to allow you to hear what he or she has to say, and to allow you to share your most private and compelling thoughts and feelings with *that partner* so that they don't become buried and torment you into getting into yet another triangle.

What, in fact, *is* the most effective means of preventing you from resorting to destructive triangles? *Exercising your ability to open up channels of communication with your primary partner.* But the "channels of communication" I want you to open involve a sense of intimacy that needs careful definition.

▲
DEFINING INTIMACY

My definition of intimacy is stimulated by the "I = Thou" concept given to us by philosopher Martin Buber. I believe, in fact, that true intimacy is impossible unless it involves an "I = Thou" relationship. What exactly is an "I = Thou" union? It's a union in which you and your partner see each other as connected, equal, spiritual beings rather than as "objects" to be manipulated (which would turn a relationship into "I = It").

The intimate union implied by this fully reciprocal "I = Thou" relationship does, however, run the risk of leading us to over-merge with the other and result in an intensity we couldn't withstand day in and day out, even if we wanted to. Our intimate associations with other people are and need to be richly varied—they involve an ebb and flow of parting and coming together which we must *allow* to happen if we're to achieve the most satisfying communion.

Destructive triangles impede this ebb and flow—they impede the necessary acceptance, even, of the *fear* we inevitably feel when we get too close to each other. Everyone feels this fear: as much as we may want to "merge" with another being, the prospect of merging often threatens our sense of boundaries, our sense of identity and self. But, paradoxically, it is through this same intimate union that you can discover and refine your unique sense of self. You can use your partner as a mirror: a mirror to see different aspects of yourself more clearly. You can use your partner as a sounding board to brainstorm new ideas and creative thoughts, as someone with whom you can live out your loving self, your passionate self, your angry self, your vulnerable self, your responsible-parent self, your "adult" self.

"Using" your partner in this way doesn't mean treating that partner as an object. You can only satisfactorily play out your various "selves" with your partner in a full, reciprocal relationship—Martin Buber's "I = Thou" union. However, as I've already said, this union depends on retreat as much as reconnection. You need, sometimes, to move out of the spiritual union of two souls to gain perspective about the outside *world* you're both in, and to remind you of your own individuality, so that you can reunite with greater strength and less fear of losing yourself. You also maintain individuality in the intimate exchange by learning how to detach from your partner while staying close. This temporary maneuver of detaching is like the natural movement of the ocean: the ebb and flow of tide washing over the "bather" (you), sometimes enveloping you, sometimes receding so that, alternately, you're engulfed, released, and engulfed again.

How can we enhance our ability to create a true "I = Thou" union? How can you engage your primary partner in a process of communication that allows each of you the kind of full, rounded "reality" true intimacy engenders? Most important, by learning to *listen* to each other more carefully than you may ever have tried to do before. I've developed a program that can help you to develop the ability really to *hear* your partner—and allow your partner, truly, to hear you. Let's focus on it right now.

▲

A SEVEN-STEP PROGRAM TO INTIMATE COMMUNICATION

You and your primary partner are always on the verge of an adventure—the extraordinary adventure of *learning more* about each other. It's perfectly normal to face this adventure with some trepidation: every "adventure" promises unanticipated discoveries, and it's human to fear the unknown. But, as I hope you've already discovered in this book, making the unknown known is an exciting process with tremendous rewards.

The following "Seven-Step Program to Intimate Communication" isn't meant to intimidate you. In fact, given the work you've already done in discovering the roots of your triangulating urges, I'm confident that you'll *enjoy* the process outlined by these seven steps. When you've achieved true "intimate communication" with your partner, you've opened up worlds for each other—you've enabled each other to experience the new *pleasure* of getting to know each other on deeper and deeper levels. In short, you've given each other the greatest gift you could: who each of you really is, inside.

Developing this intimate communion, as I suggested when I talked about Martin Buber's "I = Thou" model of intimacy before, isn't a black-and-white state of achievement. It's accepting the ebb and flow of your and your partner's feelings—accepting your occasional need to be apart from each other as well as your need to "merge" and be as close as possible. And while I stress the pleasure in the adventure of getting to know each other intimately, it's also true that each new insight you come to is usually achieved by passing through fear, fear that you "couldn't possibly" share this or that embarrassing or risky aspect of yourself—fear, however, that continually breaks down as you discover how much more of yourself you *can* share with your primary partner.

My Seven-Step Program is a "triangle buster" because, in allowing each of you to truly *hear* the other, it helps you begin to listen without judging. And when you hear each other without judging—when you hear each other in an attitude of mutual *acceptance*—you no longer feel the urge to flee to the imagined safety of a third presence. I promise that if you practice the following program with your partner, you'll prove this to yourself. However, here's a warning, to avoid frustration: these skills are simple to verbalize but difficult to accomplish. Even I who have written the seven steps, frequently need to recall them consciously as I invariably slip and find myself communicating with my husband, sons, or close friends and relatives in the language of my childhood family patterns rather than as a grown up woman.

The seven steps of achieving intimate communication are these:

1. Recognize tension.
2. Cross the street.
3. Engage the outer ear.
4. Activate the inner ear.
5. Reach for the past.
6. Share hidden meanings.
7. Build a bridge.

As we explore each of these steps in a little detail, I think you'll see how organically they grow out of all the exercises we've already done in previous chapters. Indeed, without realizing it, you've already been preparing for these steps simply by following my suggestions throughout this book. This list of steps is, in a sense, the logical outcome of all we've been working toward: letting you face your primary partner without fear, in an atmosphere of honesty, caring, and safety. You'll find, as you practice these steps, that two is infinitely better than three: your need to flee to the imagined benefits of a triangle will quite naturally dissipate and finally disappear. Practice these steps, and you'll prove this to yourself.

Here's what each of the steps amounts to.

1. *Recognize tension.*

We all betray feelings of tension in subtle ways—ways our partners learn to register, if sometimes only half-consciously. Perhaps you always reach for a cup of coffee or a newspaper when you feel tense. Perhaps your partner develops a nervous little tic—a nerve appears to "jump" in his or her eyelid, or he jangles the coins in his pocket, or she worries a lock of hair. Perhaps one or the other of you gets impossibly "cheerful"—becoming chirpy in a desperate attempt to "convince" the other that you're in a good mood. Perhaps you do the opposite, "sulking" in pointed ways you know your partner won't miss, even if he or she may say nothing about them. Reflect for a moment on some of you and your partner's tension tactics. What does your partner do that makes you realize he or she is tense? What do you do that conveys your own tension? You've done a great deal simply by acknowledging the ways that "tension" is being communicated. And when you focus especially on what makes *you* tense, you prepare yourself for the second step.

2. *Cross the street.*

Once you have learned to heighten your awareness of incipient tension in your relationship, you can learn how most effectively to respond to it. The best initial response to tension that I know is the simple one of "crossing the street." You've already seen this term in this book; it means *detaching* from a reflexive emotional reaction just at the moment of crisis—just when your "buttons" get pushed and you feel the impulse to lash out in anger or withdraw into depression because you feel your partner has provoked you. Instead, you "cross the street" to clear your mind.

Learning to cross the street means learning not to take the emotional bait you're used to snapping up—it means consciously taking a moment to give yourself "time out" so that your emotions can cool down and you can begin to *observe* you and your partner's behavior rather than immediately acting out. It is a crucial cooling-down step: you can't truly hear what your partner is saying unless you cool down. Crossing the street means giving yourself time to choose not to react, but rather to begin, with full consciousness, to *respond*. (You might imagine, for example, putting your anger "on the shelf" for five minutes while you get ready to hear your partner's side of whatever provoked you into feeling tense.)

3. *Engage the outer ear.*

Once you've crossed the street, you can begin to listen to your partner in a new way—first by doing what I call "engaging the outer ear." Engaging the outer ear simply means following the speaker's line of thinking—absorbing his or her words verbatim, as if you were a sponge. Absorbing your partner's words very carefully, without judging them, but rather simply registering them, is a skill that takes time to learn. You can keep yourself on track when you feel about to "react'" rather than listen simply by parroting your partner's statement back, in the form of a question. Let's say your partner says, "I don't think you like making love to me." You begin to feel defensive—for a moment you want to lash out with something like "Well, if it weren't for your insensitivity, your bull-headedness . . ." and you risk falling into the old rut of unproductive fighting, blame, and accusation. Instead, stop for a moment, recognize your tension, and "cross the street." Clear your mind and just repeat verbatim what your partner said so that you simply register the words: "You feel that I don't like making love to you." Then encourage your partner to continue by asking more questions—following his line of thinking literally by turning parts of his sentence, his own words, into questions. Let's say you ask your partner, "Why do you think I don't like making love to you?" He throws you with his response: "Because you always wear pajamas to bed." You can't understand why he'd make this connection, but you don't attack it as "silly." You repeat what he said in the form of a question: "Pajamas to bed? What does that mean to you?" When you turn your partner's declarative sentences into questions, it's important not to add any new thought or judgments of your own.

What you're doing is allowing the whole flow of what your partner wants to say to come out—and registering it, again without judging. This helps you two ways. First, you'll discover that what your partner says can't "destroy" you—you won't "die" (which is the common unconscious fear) if you hear all of what he or she has to say. Second, you prepare yourself for the next stage of this listening process—the stage that enables you to feel true empathy for the *meaning* of your partner's words.

4. *Activate the inner ear.*
Activating the inner ear means listening with *intuition* to sift through your partner's words so that you find the key thoughts and phrases that will convey his or her meaning to you. It too is listening without judging—but now with the aid of your imagination. Allow your mind to free-associate, absorb on a deeper level what your partner is saying. To continue our earlier imaginary example, let's say the partner turned off by pajamas explains his feelings as follows: "People only wear pajamas when they're sick." You have already taken in these words verbatim

through the "outer ear." They are now data in front of your mind's eye. Now you activate the "inner ear." "Hmm," you tell yourself, "he must have learned to associate pajamas with being sick a long time ago, and it must be a powerful lesson for him still to hold onto it." You ask, "Why do people only wear pajamas when they're sick? You're your partner's ally now—you truly want to understand, without judging, why he feels the way he does. You're also allowing imagination and your memory of what your partner may have told you in the past to open up (perhaps you know from him that his mother was over-protective whenever he got sick, making sure he was "warm" in bed even in the heat of summer). You're becoming receptive to what he's really saying, to the message behind his words. No longer is the message what your defensive self might have prodded you to believe: "He's blaming me for a lousy love life." Rather, you're acknowledging that he may be making a different association from what *you* intend to communicate when you wear pajamas.

5. *Reach for the past.*
The next step in intimate communication harks back to much of what you've already done for yourself when you diagnosed your triangles. You were able, through triangle diagrams and lists of feelings, to recall the first people and events in your life that initiated your triangle patterns. You can make some similar beneficial connections to the past with your partner. As you listen with both your "outer" and "inner" ear, registering all your partner says and allowing your intuition and imagination to tease out the meaning of what he or she is telling you, make note of key phrases or ideas. To continue the pajamas to bed example, let's say your partner says something like "When you come to bed in pajamas, I feel you are withdrawing and angry." This gives you the opportunity to allow your educated guess to be tested. "That's interesting," you might say to him. "Do you remember anyone from your past being angry at you when you were small?" You are inviting your partner to dig a lit-

tle deeper to find the source of his or her feelings—feelings your partner may have, at first glance, associated only with you but which a little judicious investigation into the past will probably reveal he or she felt many times before, with many people before you. What you're doing is allowing your partner to make connections—and also to defuse the terrible tension of feeling that "it's all your fault."

As you saw when you came up with your own root triangles, sometimes simply flashing back to the "source" can be cathartic—and healing. However, you may also have found that when you made comparisons between then and now, it became clear that the original situation was, in fact, very different from the situation you are in today. Your partner may discover this about himself or herself, too.

Let's say your husband remembers that the first time he felt anger and withdrawal was when his mother forced him to wear pajamas. He had scarlet fever and a new infant brother in the house. "My mother would always make me feel that when I was sick I did something wrong," he might say. "But it was different then than it is now. You don't scold me the way she used to. And actually, you are very kind when I get the flu or even have a cold." Your partner has discovered something very valuable: the past is *different* from now. A new realization will dawn for him as it has for you: you don't have to react now the way you did then. You have the choice to see your current circumstances in a fresh light—untethered to the patterns of your past. You have the choice to respond differently now than you did back then: you can affirm to yourself (or your partner can affirm to himself) that you've got more skills and resources today as an adult to deal with life than you did in the past as a child.

6. *Share hidden meanings.*
We all project our past behavior onto our present lives until we become *aware* that we're projecting—and that those projections are interfering with the loving connections we truly want to

make. Step 5, "Reach for the past," can go a long way to opening up that necessary awareness. Step 6 simply prods this awareness to deeper levels. Once—to continue our earlier example—your husband makes the connection to his early childhood and his feelings about his mother that pajamas equals sickness equals perceived anger, both of you can see that when he lashes out at you about this subject now, there's a "hidden" meaning behind it—or rather a meaning that is no longer hidden because, together, you've managed to find and face it. You can remind each other what's really going on when your partner lets out a familiar accusation: "Aha! There's your mother again!" This enhances intimacy in two ways: by reassuring your partner once again that the past is not the present (and that he has options available to him now he did not have then), and by reinforcing— and celebrating—the common knowledge each of you now has about the other. No longer can you "blame" each other in the old ways—now you understand too much about the sources of your feelings to lose yourself in those old, destructive fights. Step 6 establishes a rapport between you that won't easily break down.

7. *Build a bridge.*

What this entire process enables you to do is summed up by our last step: building a bridge from that first moment of tension where both of you feel "attacked" to point of considering real solutions to that tension. You're able to reach this point now because you've given each other reassurance, first, that it's okay for each of you to feel what you feel; second, that it's possible for each of you to *examine* what you feel in a way that won't threaten either of you; third, that you can use the *insights* you derive from that examination in some productive ways right now.

The rewards of this process aren't only that you can hear your partner in a new, more productive way, but that you can now *talk* to your partner in your partner's own language. What, in fact, you're both doing when you submit to these seven steps is teaching each other your separate vocabularies: you're letting each other know how you think and feel, in terms that express your thought and feelings best. Anger is now a foreign tongue you've left behind. Now that you've created a receptive, intimate, *safe* environment to share what each of you feels, you can begin to weigh pros and cons of solutions. You can begin to change your behavior to something that accommodates both of you, or simply *say* things in a way that won't alienate either of you. "I don't think you like to make love to me," for example, can become "What's wrong? Is there anything I can do to lessen the distance between us so that we can be physically close again? My own feelings about pajamas is that when I wear them on winter evenings, it reminds me of being safe and cozy at home. Rather than feeling turned off, I feel even more ready for sex because I feel so well cared for." Usually, after such a dialog there is a change or compromise made, often without further discussion being necessary. After the pajamas dialog, for example, the wearer is less likely to wear them and the speaker is also less likely to be hurt should they be worn. The interchange between a couple magically softens and the content becomes less important to both people.

Building a bridge means building a two-way bridge—one each of you can use to listen to and understand the other. In fact, an interesting fact about this whole Seven-Step Program is that it can be a simple test of whether you're in a relationship that has any hope of going forward. If one or both of you resist this process, it generally indicates one of two things. Either one of you is too attached to childhood family issues to even begin to take a look at them (outside therapeutic help is a good idea in this case), or one or both of you have already moved out of the relationship and are already on to something—or someone—else.

If you know you are not resisting this program, yet it is not working very well, please have patience with yourself. Remember, it still to this very day takes a big effort on my part to use the seven steps when I feel tension with my significant other. Allow yourself time to begin to really use this process.

▲

TOWARD A NEW FREEDOM

Sometimes, as we've seen before in this book, the urge to triangulate can mask the genuine urge to leave the relationship you're in—it can mask the fact that you truly do not feel you're with the right "primary partner." It takes courage to acknowledge this—to face the fact that you're engineering the breakup of your relationship by turning to a third presence (or allowing your partner to turn to that third presence). It takes even greater courage to resist the triangulating urge and decide to confront your partner about your feelings directly. But the rewards of direct confrontation are—at least eventually—great. You're paving your way to a freedom you can achieve in no other way. You're acknowledging that who you are and what you want are important, and that you deserve the right to pursue the life and relationship you want to pursue.

More often, however, triangles mask what we've seen in this book again and again: a crippling fear of intimacy. The ways in which you may have prevented yourself from experiencing the intimacy you crave can be baffling at first sight, as we've seen in all of the Love Triangle's permutations. But you now have tools to begin to understand why and how you've prevented yourself from achieving intimacy. Using these tools can lead you to an unprecedented view of yourself—and a feeling of freedom you may never have realized was possible.

The freedom you can find with your partner by following the triangle techniques and intimate-communication program you've learned in this book is profoundly exhilarating and healing. But you'll discover something perhaps even more important than the fact that you're able to share honestly with your partner, with a new feeling of safety and caring. You'll discover that it's all right to be exactly who you are now—to have all the feelings, doubts, fears, anxieties, memories, joys, and insights that make you the person you are. You'll discover you don't need to run away anymore. When, out of your old conditioning and fears, triangles beckon to you again, you'll not only have the tools to resist their attraction, but, as you practice using those tools, your strength in resisting old patterns will grow. You'll be developing something most triangulators never dream of experiencing: a feeling of true self-sufficiency.

Not only will you have developed the ability to face your primary partner "head on," without resorting to a triangle, but you'll be able to face all of the rest of your life that way, too. That's the goal of everything we've explored in this book. While the hard truth is that reaching this goal means facing up to some of your deepest fears, the happy news is that you've now learned a way to do it that won't threaten you. You've learned it's safe to be honest with yourself and with your partner about what's really bothering you. You've learned that you don't *need* triangles anymore.

The rewards this knowledge offers are immeasurable. The process of untangling your triangles goes far beyond giving you a chance at real love. It can give you the chance of a full, free, and satisfying life.

ABOUT THE AUTHORS

Bonnie Jacobson, Ph.D., has been in psychology since 1963. In the early seventies, she cofounded two training institutes—one for psychotherapeutic treatment and the second serving Wall Street investment firms through the medium of workshops. In the 1980s, she founded The New York Institute for Psychological Change. Her first book was called *The Change Process*. Her second book, *How to Listen to the Ones You Love: The Path to Lifelong Intimacy*, led, logically, into this present book, *Love Triangles*. She is married, has two grown sons, and lives in New York City.

Guy Kettelhack is the coauthor of more than a dozen nonfiction books, including *On a Clear Day You Can See Yourself* with Dr. Sonya Friedman, *How to Love a Nice Guy* with Dr. Judith Kuriansky, and *Easing the Ache*, which he did under the pseudonym David Crawford. He lives in New York City.